SELF-DEFENSE
for WOMEN

How to Stay Safe and Fight Back

This book is dedicated to my sister, Judy.

SELF-DEFENSE
for WOMEN

How to Stay Safe and Fight Back

SUSAN L. PETERSON

LEISURE PRESS

NEW YORK

A publication of
Leisure Press.
597 Fifth Avenue: New York, N.Y. 10017

Library of Congress Cataloging in Publication Data

Peterson, Sue (Susan L.)
Self-defense for women

1. Self-defense for women. I. Title.
GV1111.5.P46 1984 613.6'6'088042 82.80784
ISBN 0-88011-114-3

Text photographs by: Robert W. Caudy
     David Madison
     Tim Davis
     Peter Belsito

Cover photographs: Front: David Madison
     Back: Robert W. Caudy

Contents

5007973

1

Why Self-Defense?

Every woman wants to look good and feel terrific. Along with the obvious components of physical fitness—muscular strength, muscular endurance, flexibility, and cardio-respiratory endurance—women must add one more element vital for general well-being: self-defense. Self-defense is self-confidence, born of familiarity with skills and the knowledge that in a given situation you will be able to defend yourself to the best of your capabilities.

Given the dramatic increase in the number of rapes, muggings and other violent crimes involving women in the United States, every woman is forced to assume a greater degree of responsibility for her own personal safety. In a country where a crime is committed every few minutes, a woman needs to learn self-defense. In fact, at any time in your lifetime, any one of you may become a victim of a crime—whether it be verbal or sexual harassment, robbery, assault, rape or murder. After teaching self-defense classes for 15 years, consulting with numerous victims of rape and muggings, talking with police officers, working with military experts in combatives, I have discovered that these women who have been victimized all seemed to have only one thing in common . . . they were vulnerable! They were all in the wrong place at the wrong time. Myths about women being raped or assaulted because they dressed or acted in a sexy, provocative manner just are not true. There does not seem to be a "typical" victim. She may be any age from infant to grandmother; she may be very beautiful or totally unattractive; she may be dressed in an evening gown or in old jeans; she may be thin or fat; and she may be attacked in her home, in her car, on the street or in an elevator. I repeat, any woman may become a victim of a crime, and every woman needs to practice self-defense.

THE FIRST LESSON IN SELF-DEFENSE: PREVENTION

Unfortunately, with crime statistics the way they are, you must change the way in which you live your life. You should install proper locks on all doors and windows in your house, and you may even need an alarm system. You should not walk alone at night, perhaps even in your own neighborhood. You should not open your doors unless the caller identifies himself first or is expected. When out alone, you should dress casually to discourage muggers. You should leave lights, a radio or a television set on at home when you are gone for the evening. You should check back with a friend's house to say you arrived home safely. And so on. These are all methods of preventing a crime. Your first lesson in self-defense is to prevent a crime before it happens. Avoid potential danger and never become a victim. Chapter 2 of this book is devoted to this first, very important lesson: prevention.

DIFFERENT TYPES OF SELF-DEFENSE

A woman who avoids her assailant, or who talks her way out of a potential assault, is obviously less vulnerable to injury than a woman who is forced to defend herself against an adversary who, in most instances, will be larger and stronger than she. Whatever the method, you should be prepared to defend yourself in some way . . . whether it be talking or physically fighting!

Women have been very successful in talking their way out of an attack situation. However, this seems to work best when you have given it some prior thought and in fact already have a story prepared. You must be a good actress and very convincing. If you don't think you will be able to tell such a story under what will be a lot of stress, do not attempt to do so. Several of my students have shared their most successful stories with me: "I have a terminal disease with only days to live" (e.g., brain tumor, cancer, etc.); "I have a contagious disease" (e.g., VD, herpes, etc.); "I have a very sick child at home who will suffer horribly if I don't get home immediately"; "I am pregnant"; "I just had 'female' surgery and will bleed profusely." Talking may also momentarily distract the assailant so that other, more direct types of self-defense may be used.

Another type of self-defense is to make noise—yell loudly or scream for help. Nothing is written that says you must fight or defend yourself alone. If you are in fact someplace where your cries for assistance might be heard, then by all means, scream out with all your heart and soul! A countless number of women have saved their own lives by screaming for help. Yelling is also a great distraction; it may easily startle the attacker and cause him to halt his assault momentarily. This pause may then permit you to use other appropriate self-defense techniques to help along your escape. The only time you would not want to startle your assailant by screaming is if he is holding a weapon on you. Noise may then frighten him into using the weapon to silence you immediately.

When yelling out for assistance, the word to use is "FIRE" — not "HELP" or "RAPE." Unfortunately, so many people these days are afraid to get involved with someone else's problems, that they may not respond to cries for help. Yell "FIRE," however, and people are fearful that their own home or family is endangered. Doors and windows open, people appear on the streets, the fire and/or police department is called and you have a real chance of being helped.

Screaming requires practice. Scream into a pillow at home, or in the car while driving to work. Screaming is not natural for all women. In fact, if you already know that you would not be able to scream in an emergency, then carry a whistle. Several of my students have told of their experience of being grabbed or mugged on the street and to their horror not being able to utter a sound when they opened their mouths to scream. This is not unusual, so be prepared to blow a whistle. Buy an inexpensive metal whistle (the loudest you can find) and carry it with you at all times. Put it on your key chain and have it ready *in your hand* whenever you find you are in a potentially dangerous situation. Also practice blowing the whistle so that you will be able to make as much noise as possible.

The last type of self-defense is to fight back physically. However, you should use these skills only after you have tried all the other methods first, and your only choice left is to fight back. And you must be ready to fight without hesitation and with total confidence in your skills. Never even attempt to fight unless you are committed to fight with 100% of everything you know. You must be prepared mentally and physically. You are ready to hurt your assailant and protect your own life.

Obviously, not all women are capable of physically fighting back. You need to ask yourself if you would in fact be ready to fight for your life. Know yourself. Women generally do not like to think about the possibility of having to defend themselves. It is much easier to hope that someone will be there to help you—a spouse, friend or relative. But you must think about being victimized. We know that any preparation or pre-thought at all helps reduce your chances of becoming a victim in the first place—you are more apt to avoid danger when you have considered the consequences. A woman who cannot admit to herself that "yes, it could happen to me," has a much more difficult time reacting defensively when an attack does occur.

Think about how you would react to an actual attack situation. Would it be best for you to try to talk your way out of an attack? Are you adequately prepared to fight? Have you ever been in a fight? Have you taken a self-defense course? Have you practiced lately? Are you confident enough about your skills to be able to use them successfully? Will you panic?

Reading this book isn't enough. I encourage all women to take some sort of self-defense or combatives classes. You will learn a lot about yourself. Perhaps you are the type of woman who has never experienced any hostile, physical type of contact. You have never been aggressively grabbed, pushed or handled. No one has ever hit or slapped you. A properly taught self-defense class can pretty well simulate this type of physical attacking which often occurs on the street. It would be important for you to know how you would react to such a situation—not that I am saying you must be hit by your self-defense instructor! If you are interested in taking a class in self-defense, contact your local police department for a recommended course or program. You might also want to check with local schools and colleges in your area to see if they offer such classes. Ask other women for recommended courses—local YWCA's, recreation centers or community women centers. There are often several quality courses taught at fair rate's right in your own community.

No matter what form of self-defense you use, most criminals do not expect a woman to defend herself in any manner, and so you have the advantage of the element of surprise. This may buy you precious time to escape or actually hurt your assailant before he can attack you further. In addition, an attacker who sees that he has to fight his victim may flee in hopes of finding an easier mark! So, surprise your attacker—react quickly, skillfully and with confidence that you will in fact be able to defend yourself.

The initial step in the struggle for survival is to commit yourself to doing everything possible to lead a long and injury-free life. Undeniably, this commitment begins with the learning of techniques for self-defense, so turn now to Chapter 2, and begin the program that may save your life. Don't delay. The urban jungle is becoming more dangerous every day!

2

Prevention

The first lesson of self-defense is to prevent a crime before it happens. Many crimes can be prevented if you use some very common sense measures and simple safeguards. This chapter discusses safety for you while in your home, in your car and on the street. Before you learn any specific physical skills for fighting an attacker, you must first learn how to *avoid* dangerous situations which would require the use of such skills.*

PERSONAL SAFETY

An attacker will most often select a victim who appears to be vulnerable, who looks as if she would be easy to control or overpower physically. So, avoid becoming a victim by being conscious of how you look and act at all times. Dress appropriately. Wear comfortable clothing and, if possible, shoes which would enable you to run or move quickly if need be. More and more working women are wearing their sneakers and carrying their high heels in a gym bag on their way to and from their jobs. Have confidence in your physical, as well as mental, capabilities and stamina. Walk in a well-postured manner with your head held high. Always be alert to your surroundings and be aware of the people around you. Do not daydream while waiting for the bus or walking to lunch—look around and notice people, places

---

*Do not be offended at how *obvious* many of these preventive measures actually are. Many crimes happen because the victim has ignored the obvious, e.g., locking her front door but forgetting to lock the back door of her house!

and things. Try to remain calm if actually confronted with a danger-ous situation. Don't panic. Whenever there is a possibility of attack, be prepared mentally, as well as physically. Know ahead of time exactly what you would do in a specific hazardous situation. Know what defenses you are going to use, remember that you have already given this possibility some thought and you are ready!

Although I do not advocate carrying any lethal weapons on your person (other than your own hands and feet!), there are several items typically found in a woman's purse which could very easily be used to aid you in self-defense. A few examples are as follows:

- comb: stab eyes or throat; scrape face
- brush: jab pointed end to throat; hit groin
- keys: stab eyes; stab throat
- pen or pencil (or metal nail file): jab or stab at the face or back of the hand
- hairspray or breath spray: spray into eyes
- whistle: blow to call for assistance
- entire purse: sling or throw it at the assailant

Remember that the only time any of these purse weapons would be helpful to you is if they are held ready in your hand when needed — not lying somewhere in the bottom of your purse.

Examples of items which are frequently found in a woman's purse which could very easily be used to aid the woman in her self-defense.

SAFETY AT HOME

Many crimes occur in the victim's house. The following precautions should be taken for safety there:

1. Keep your doors locked at all times—whether home or not. You would be amazed at the tremendous number of burglaries which occur without forced entry, where the burglar just walked in through an unlocked door.
2. Use strong, secure locks. The best is a deadbolt that requires a key(s) both inside and outside. When you are home, lock the bolt from the inside but do not leave the key in the lock. Hide it where you and others living in the house can get to it quickly if there is an emergency. Spring locks, which lock automatically when you close the door, are easy to pick. Use a chain lock and if possible a peephole in the door. Be sure to check to see who is at the door *before* opening it. Again, you would be surprised at the large number of attackers who are let into their victims' homes through the front door!
3. Lock and secure all windows and screens (even in summer). Be especially careful about windows which are accessible at the street or ground floor level.
4. In high crime neighborhoods, more and more people are putting metal bars on their windows and doors. Although a deterrant, even these can be removed if the bolts securing them are on the outside. In addition, these may be very dangerous in an emergency (fire, for example) where escape must be quick, especially if you have small children.
5. If you use a telephone answering machine, do not leave a recorded message which states that you are not at home. Say that you cannot come to the phone at the moment and will return the call as soon as possible. A potential burglar calling your home to see if anyone is home would appreciate your open invitation.
6. If you live alone, do not put your name on your mail box—once someone has your name and address, getting your phone number is fairly easy. Also, list only your last name and first initial in the phone directory. In addition, many women no longer list their address in the phone directory.
7. Keep shades, blinds and curtains closed—especially when dressing. As ridiculous as this warning may sound, interviews with rapists have revealed that many had seen their victims through bare windows.
8. If alone, never admit a stranger into your home. Ask to see appropriate identification for a salesman, repairman

and/or delivery man—even if he is expected and in uniform. If necessary, make a phone call to check if that person was actually sent to your home. If you are home alone with a repairman, you might make him think that someone is expected home "at any minute." Another check for a "phony" repairman is to see if the appropriate company car is parked in front of your house—he may have the right uniform but the wrong car. Be careful if a repairman comes to your home because of a report of a problem by a neighbor. Check this out. One of my students let a repairman into her apartment because he said her downstairs neighbor had complained about a water leak from my student's kitchen. He was a phony, and luckily my student had a roommate who came home at the right time!

9. If a stranger comes to your door and asks to use the phone, ask for the number and you call while he waits outside.

10. Make sure that all entrances to your home are well lighted. When returning home at night, be sure a light is on at that entrance. You may also want to install an automatic timer to turn lights on at dusk when you are away from home. That way there will be lights on when you return home, and burglars do not like lights! More and more people are leaving their front porch lights on all night.

11. Do not make it known to someone that you will be home alone on a particular night, such as when your roommate or husband is out of town. If someone does knock at the door, make him think you are *not* alone. Yell, "John, get the door, I'm busy," or "My husband will be with you in a minute," and so on.

12. Be careful in choosing where to hide an extra key. Burglars know to look under the doormat or on the ledge above the door. Also, be smart about where you hide your valuables at home. The master bedroom is usually the first room searched. Dresser drawers, cabinets, purses, pockets, and the locked jewelry box are also not very good hiding places. Try hiding valuables in containers in cluttered closets or cupboards, in with the dirty laundry, in covered pots and pans, or in packages of food in the refrigerator.

13. If you live in a high crime rate area, install alarm warning devices. Be sure to have plenty of decals on windows and doors to announce the presence of the alarm system. Burglars do not like noise! Another noise-maker is a dog with a loud bark. Just a house pet will do; you don't need to buy a "killer" dog.

14. Keep a phone beside the bed or within easy reach at night. Know whether or not your area has the use of the 911

emergency phone number to summon police. Otherwise, know the number of your local police department. Post it near the phone.

15. When returning home at night, have your keys unobtrusively out in your hand before reaching the door. Do not be fumbling at your doorstep looking for the house key while loaded down with groceries or packages. Once inside the house, close and lock the door.

16. If upon returning home you suspect a prowler is inside, leave and get help. Do not enter alone. In addition, be observant as you approach your front door. Notice if the door is still locked, the lights on as left, if things generally are as you left them. One of my "senior" students who lives in an apartment building in a large city rings her doorbell and waits a few minutes before she enters . . . to give the burglar time to escape!

17. If you are inside your home and you hear someone else in the house, quickly call the police or even the fire department for help. If you actually wake up in the middle of the night and see someone in your bedroom, what should you do? Police generally react differently to this question. Of course, if a weapon is visible, cooperate as best you can— chances are good that all he wants are your valuables and he will take them and then leave. If there is a weapon or not, some police officers say to pretend you are asleep and let him take your valuables and leave. Others say to turn on the lights, scream and yell, throw things and make such a commotion that you will frighten the burglar and cause him to run. In fact, I have had several students in my classes who have reacted in just this way, and the burglars did run! Also, talk with your neighbors so that they know to call the police if they hear all this racket in the middle of the night.

18. If you're on vacation or away for a couple of days, secure the house and stop all regular deliveries if possible. Ask a neighbor to pick up the mail, tend the yard if necessary and generally look after the house. You may also want your neighbor or friend to actually "use" your house while you are gone—go inside and watch TV, cook a meal, wash their car in your driveway, etc. If this is not possible, use an automatic timer to turn lights, radios or TV on and off at different times of the day or evening when such things would be normal if you were home. Finally, turn down the bell on your telephone so the numerous rings can not be heard on the street.

19. Organize a crime prevention—neighborhood watch program in your community. Help one another look out for

each other's property. Call your local police department for details. I actually encourage my neighbors to be "nosey".

20. If you receive a harassing or obscene phone call:
   - Hang up immediately and quietly. Don't slam down the receiver and let the caller know that you are upset—that is generally the reaction he wants.
   - If calls continue, notify the police and/or phone company. A new, unlisted number can be given to you free of charge for 30 days in most areas.
   - Do not try to counsel or help the caller.
   - Do not give your number to a person who says he has the wrong number. Ask what number he wants and say, "No, this is not the number you wanted," and then hang up.
   - Do not let the caller know your name or that you are alone if you are.
   - Warn children not to give out names, numbers or other information to strangers on the phone.

If you receive a harassing or obscene phone call, don't let the caller know your name or that you are alone if you are.

SAFETY IN THE CAR

The following precautions should be taken:

1. Keep all doors and windows closed and locked. If a window must be opened, open it on the driver's side only just enough for air. Keep your purse and any packages on the floor or out of sight. In many large cities, women have had their purses grabbed from the front seat of their car through an open door or window while waiting at a stoplight.

2. Use well-lighted streets and thoroughfares. Do not take shortcuts on unknown roads, or on lonely roads without travelers' services.

3. Always keep your parked car locked. Park in areas that will be well lighted when you return to your car. Have your key ready in your hand and check the front and rear seats of the car to be sure no one is hiding inside before you enter. Try to park close to a building or residence if you will be returning to your car late at night. One of my students was grabbed in a school parking lot while walking to her car after a late night class. When she had arrived at school earlier in the day, the lot had been full and she did not even notice how far away from the gym she had to park.

4. Do not pick up hitchhikers!

5. Before departing on a trip, be sure that everything is in working order — and that you have plenty of gas, water, a spare tire and flares. Also, know your route and carry maps in case you do get lost. After getting lost with very little gas in the car in downtown Chicago late one night, I always check to see how much gas is in the car as soon as I get in!

6. If the car breaks down, put on your flashers, raise the hood and remain in the locked car. If a motorist stops to help, ask him to call the police or a tow truck. Do *not* get out of the car, day or night—some would-be assailants purposely cause minor auto accidents just to get you out of your car. If in doubt, stay in the car and wait for the police to arrive.

7. Do not leave your keys with a parking attendant (your car key as well as any other key on the ring may be duplicated in a very short time). If you must leave the car keys, leave only the ignition key. Put any valuables in the car in the trunk or out of sight as much as possible. Do not mark your key ring with your name, address or phone number. I had a student who parked in a public attendant-operated parking lot for the day while she went shopping. She left her key ring with her house key on it in the car. Someone got her home address from her car registration, which was in the car glove compartment, took her house key and burglarized

her home while she was shopping. She did not even miss her house key until she arrived home.

8. If you believe you are being followed, drive to a police station, fire station or gas station. Stay in your car and honk your horn until someone comes out to help you. By all means, do not drive home, to your sister's or to your girl-friend's house!

9. If you get home and discover you have been followed, stay in the locked car. Either park and blow the horn, or drive to safety if possible. Again, do not leave the car.

10. Always carry change in your car for an emergency phone call.

Keep all doors and windows closed and locked.

SAFETY ON THE STREET

When walking outside day or night, the following precautions should be taken:

1. If at all possible, avoid walking alone—especially at night. If you get stuck without a ride, ask a friend to walk with or take you home. Always try to have extra cash for a cab, even if it is only a few blocks.

2. If you must walk alone, walk briskly and with confidence. Try to wear shoes and clothing suitable for walking. Be alert and aware of your surroundings. Remember, a potential rapist can tell a lot about the vulnerability of a woman by the way she is walking.

3. Walk through familiar neighborhoods and on familiar streets. Go where there are street lights, businesses and people. Avoid taking shortcuts or using alleyways, and steer clear of doorways. Walk toward the middle of a sidewalk, away from buildings. Stay away from curbs if there are parked cars. If at night, and you are particularly fearful of an area, walk down the middle of the street—especially if you think you are being followed!

4. *Never* hitchhike or accept a ride from someone you do not know well (male or female).

5. If at all possible, try to ignore catcalls, whistles or other verbal remarks. Often hecklers are just trying to get some kind of reaction from you. Personally, I try to avoid jogging past construction work sites.

6. If someone in a car asks for directions, keep a safe distance from the person. Call out directions if you desire, but do not walk over to the car and possibly get grabbed or pulled inside the car.

7. Carry change on you for a phone call, and try to notice the location of the police call boxes on the streets.

8. If you think you are being followed, make sure. Cross the street, change directions, or enter a business or gas station. If you have no other choice, walk towards a home or apartment building with lights on.

9. If you decide that you are in fact being followed, stay where you are if you have entered a shop or gas station. Otherwise, scream or blow your whistle for help if assistance is near. Since the majority of women would not be able to outrun their assailant, run from him only if help is near or you have someplace to run to. A personal goal should be for you to be able to run at least two city blocks.

10. Finally, if you are being followed and assistance is definitely not near, stop and face the assailant in a good defen-

To avoid purse snatchers, you should carry your purse close to your body or under your arm.

sive stance and be prepared to fight. If a weapon is not visible, speak out in a loud, aggressive, and confident voice, "What do you want from me?" or "Are you following me?" Not appearing to be vulnerable or an "easy mark" may be enough for the potential assailant to leave you alone. In addition, it may just be some businessman from out of town lost and looking for his hotel!

11. If you are being followed by a car, turn around to walk quickly in the opposite direction. Enter a store, cafe or gas station and tell someone that you are being followed.

12. Keep your hands as free as possible on the street. Never overload yourself with packages. If you must defend yourself, drop everything—even your purse.

13. To avoid muggers and purse snatchers:

     • Carry your purse close to your body or under your arm—not hanging loosely off your shoulder. Better yet, do not even carry a purse. Have your money or identification in your pockets or in a container smaller than a purse, such as a credit card holder.

     • Do not carry all your money in your purse or in your wallet—distribute it around your person. Do not carry any more cash than you absolutely need. Some people think that they should carry some cash so that they have something to give to the mugger.

     • Do not leave your purse unattended—for example, sitting on a lunch counter, or in a shopping basket, hanging on the back of a door of a public restroom, or hooked on the back of your chair in a restaurant.

     • Do not publicly display money. Count your change or any money received in the store or bank before you go back out onto the street.

     • Plan ahead. If you know you may be walking in a potentially dangerous area, do not wear expensive jewelry. Leave your best watch, earrings, even your wedding ring, at home that night.

14. If someone attempts to rob you and has a weapon, don't be a heroine. If he asks for your valuables, immediately give him what he wants. Do not hesitate—people have been shot by a nervous robber because it took too long to remove their watch or ring. Try to notice as much as you can about the robber, and report the crime to the police as soon as possible—no matter how little may have been taken. Do not be embarrassed or blame yourself for being victimized. Report the crime so you can perhaps prevent someone else from becoming a victim!

3

Fitness and Self-Defense*

A self-defense program for women is not realistic or complete unless physical fitness is a part of it. If you hope to learn, practice and successfully use (when necessary) the self-defense skills found in this book, you should be physically fit. Although numerous definitions of fitness exist, in the case of self-defense, physical fitness is the capacity of an individual to successfully meet a *physical* challenge. At the minimum, a physically fit woman should possess a reasonably high level of each of the basic components of fitness: cardiovascular fitness, flexibility and muscular fitness. Cardiovascular fitness is the ability of the body to continue prolonged activity while resisting fatigue. Flexibility refers to an increased range of motion of the skeletal joints of the body, which allows improved movement. Muscular fitness is the capacity of the body to exert force against resistance. Without these basic components of physical fitness, you have considerably less of a chance of successfully warding off the average male attacker.

The following exercises are designed to improve and contribute to the basic components of personal fitness. Physical exercise and

---

*Exercises found in this chapter were taken from the following books: The Woman's Stretching Book by Susan L. Peterson, (Leisure Press, New York, 1983); The Sexy Stomach by James A. Peterson, Ph.D., and Susan L. Peterson (Leisure Press, New York, 1983); Sexy Legs by James A. Peterson, Ph.D., and Susan L. Peterson, (Leisure Press, New York, 1983); and Sexy Buttocks by James A. Peterson, Ph.D., and Susan L. Peterson (Leisure Press, New York, 1983).

activity should be an integral part of every woman's daily life. It may take many forms: individual lifetime sports, such as tennis, golf and racquetball; recreational exercising, such as jogging, swimming, and bicycling; or, finally, specific developmental exercising, such as calisthenics.

A developmental exercise program should be performed at least three to four times a week, and more frequently if possible. A workout should last a least fifteen to twenty minutes. Prior to beginning any type of exercise program, a *physician* should be consulted regarding the ability of the individual to engage in the proposed exercise program.

In some instances, an extensive physical examination may be necessary before the exercise program commences. A developmental workout should give attention to all three major components of physical fitness. In order to ensure that the individual has a proper foundation of fitness, the workouts and conditioning efforts can be segmented into three levels of performance: beginner, intermediate and advanced. The beginner's level of exercise is for the woman who is just starting an exercise program, the intermediate level is for someone who has been doing some form of regular exercise or physical activity, and the advanced exercises are for the woman who exercises vigorously almost daily.

CARDIOVASCULAR FITNESS

This type of exercise must be vigorous enough to require both the heart and lungs to work at a greater-than-resting level of efficiency. Physical activities, such as running, jogging, swimming, jumping, skipping rope and/or bicycling, are large-muscle activities that will help you develop your level of cardiovascular fitness. The following specific exercises will also contribute to muscular endurance and should be performed as warmups prior to doing flexibility and strength type exercises.

Beginner

1. Run in place 50 counts (25 counts on each foot) with your hands on your hips or your arms bent loosely at the elbows, raising your knees up waist high. Continue with 10 jumping jacks—from a standing position, with your legs together, jump with your legs apart and your hands clapping overhead, and return to the start by bringing your legs together again as your hands slap your thighs. Relax and

Exercise which is designed to improve your level of cardiovascular fitness must be vigorous enough to require both your heart and lungs to work at a greater-than-resting level of efficiency.

repeat 50 counts running in place and 10 jumping jacks.

or

2. Jump with your hands on your hips and your feet together first forward, then backward, to the right, and to the left. Repeat this series in that order 15 to 20 times. Relax and repeat the sequence once again.

Intermediate

1. Run in place 100 counts; continue with 15 jumping jacks. Relax and repeat the sequence once again.

or

2. Jump forward, backward, right and left 50 counts. Relax and repeat once again.

or

3. Jump rope in place with your feet together 100 counts. Relax and repeat once again.

Cardiovascular Fitness: Jump Rope

Advanced

1. Run in place 2 or 3 minutes. Relax, repeat once again.
   or
2. Jump rope 2 or 3 minutes. Relax, repeat once again.
   or
3. Do combination jumping jacks: Do a jumping jack, then quickly kick the right leg up high to the left while clapping your hands together under your leg, quickly repeat the kick with your left leg to the right and clap your hands. Do this combination 20 times. Relax and repeat the sequence once again.

Cardiovascular Fitness: Combination Jumping Jacks

Flexibility

The following flexibility exercises concentrate on stretching the back, trunk, legs, arms and shoulders. The exercises are performed slowly and smoothly. Each static stretch is held 6-10 seconds. Do not bounce while doing these exercises. Stretching exercises should be done prior to strengthening type exercises.

Beginner (Perform each of the following exercises 6-8 times.)

1. Seated — Legs Together: Sit with your legs together, and slowly bend forward from the hips and try to touch your hands to your ankles. Keep your head up. If you can't reach your ankles, go as far as you can. Each day you'll improve—that is invariably true with flexibility exercises, and is applicable to all that follows in this section. Hold the stretch 6-10 seconds. Relax, repeat.

Seated—Legs Together

2. Seated — Legs Apart: Sit with your legs apart. Turn to the right, lean forward from your hips and try to touch your hands to your feet. Then reach center with both hands and try to touch the floor; and finally, turn to the left and touch. Return to the start, relax and repeat reaching right, center, left, etc.

Seated—Legs Apart: Side Reach

Seated—Legs Apart: Center Reach

3. Frog Sit: Sit with the soles of your feet together while grasping your feet with your hands. Pull your upper body forward towards your feet. Keep your head up. Do not round your shoulders. Hold, relax and repeat.

Frog Sit

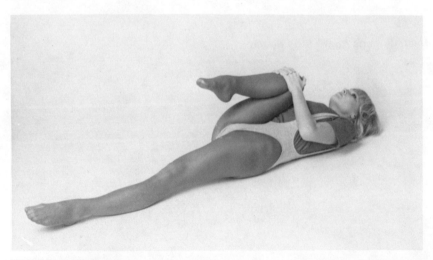

Chest-Knee Pull

4. Chest-Knee Pull: Lie on your back. Bring one knee up to your chest and pull it in against your stomach. Return the knee to the start and repeat with the other knee. Repeat in succession.

5. Arm Flings: Sit with your legs crossed and your back straight. Bend your arms and hold them up at shoulder level, with your fingertips just about touching. Now pull your bent arms backward 3 times on 3 counts, and on the 4th count fling the arms and elbows extended fully backward. Repeat the sequence. Keep your arms up at shoulder level throughout the exercise.

Arm Flings: Arms Bent

Arm Flings: Arm Back

Intermediate and Advanced (Perform each of the following exercises 8 to 10 times unless otherwise instructed.)

1. Standing Toe Touch: Stand with your legs together and your knees slightly bent. Bend forward and downward at the waist and touch your toes with both hands. Hold, relax and repeat.

Standing Toe Touch

2. Standing Ankle Touch—Legs Apart: Stand with your legs apart. Turn to your right and touch both your hands to your right anklebone and hold. Move to the center and touch both hands to the floor and hold. Move to the left and touch and hold. Return upright and repeat right, center, left, etc.

Standing Ankle Touch

Single-Leg Crossover

3. Single Leg Crossover: Lie on your back with your arms held out at your shoulders. Lift your right leg up toward the ceiling and slowly cross it over to your left to touch the floor up by your left hand. Hold, return your leg to the center and the starting position. Repeat the crossover with your other leg. Repeat in succession right, left, etc.

4. Arm Circles: Stand with your arms at your sides. Slowly circle your right arm 10 counts forward and 10 counts backward. Repeat with your left arm and then both arms together. Relax and repeat the sequence once. Describe as large and as true a circle as possible with each count.

Arm Circles—One Arm Backward   **Arm Circles—Both Arms Backward**

Shoulder Squeeze

5. Shoulder Squeeze: Sit with both your arms behind your back and your hands grasped together. Now squeeze (draw) your shoulder blades together. Hold, relax and repeat.

MUSCULAR FITNESS

The following muscular fitness exercises concentrate on the abdominal, leg/hips, and arm/shoulder girdle areas. These body areas generally lack firmness and muscle tonus. The exercises are performed slowly and smoothly. Generally, these exercises will be performed with 2 counts for an upward movement, and 4 counts for a downward movement. These exercises are to be done after your warmup and flexibility exercises.

Beginner (Perform each of the following exercises 6-8 times):

1. Abdominal:
    a. Curl-ups: Lie on your back, with your knees slightly bent, and with your arms held down by your sides. Slowly curl your head forward (tucking your chin to your chest), reaching your arms toward your feet, and continue curling upward until your head and shoulders are off the floor. Pause and slowly uncurl downward. Relax and repeat.

Curl-up   **Hip Roll**

    b. Hip Roll: Lie on your back with your arms held out at your sides. Slowly bring both knees up to your chest, roll right with your knees pointed toward your elbow and lower your knees until they are 1-2 inches from the floor. Hold, return to center, roll left and hold, return to center and extend your legs to the starting position. Relax and repeat the sequence. Keep your head, shoulders and upper back on the floor as much as possible while rolling.

2. Legs and Hips:
   a. Hand-Knee Leg Lifts: Kneeling on your hands and knees, extend your right leg backward along the floor and slowly lift it up 10-12 inches. Hold and slowly lower it. Repeat in succession. Repeat with your left leg. Do not lift your legs higher than your hips.

Hand-Knee Leg Lift

Side Leg Lift

   b. Side Leg Lifts: Lie on your side with one leg on top of the other. Slowly lift one leg up 8-10 inches only and hold; then slowly lower the leg. Repeat in succession. Roll onto your other side and repeat with the other leg. Try to keep your body in as straight a line as possible while lifting.

3. Arms and Shoulders:
   a. Isometric Pull and Push: Sit comfortably with your arms held out in front of you at chest level and your elbows bent. Hook your fingers together and pull one hand against the other as hard as possible for 6 to 10 seconds. Relax and shake loose. Then place the heels of your hands together with fingers extended in opposite directions and push hard together for 6 to 10 seconds. Shake hands loose and repeat the pull and push sequence.

Isometric Pull

Isometric Push

b. Wall Push: Stand approximately an arm's distance from a wall with your hands placed on the wall at or just above eye level with your fingertips touching. Keep your heels on the floor and your body straight. Now move your body toward the wall with your arms bending until your forehead touches your hands. Push against the wall and extend your arms, moving your body slowly backwards to the starting position. Relax and repeat. For a real challenge, try to do the push off the wall with only one arm placed on the wall. Alternate right arm only, left arm, right, etc.

Wall Push

Wall Push: One Arm Only

Intermediate (Perform each of the following exercises 8-12 times unless otherwise instructed):

1. Abdominals:
   a. Sit-ups: Lie on your back with your knees bent and your hands clasped behind your head. Slowly curl forward and upward until your chest touches your knees, and then uncurl slowly backward to the start. Repeat.

Sit-Ups

Bicycle Sequence

   b. Bicycle Sequence: Lie on your back supporting yourself up on your elbows. Lift both your legs up off the floor (only 12-15 inches) and slowly move your legs in a bicycle pedaling fashion. Relax and repeat. Do not arch your lower back while pedaling!

2. Legs and Hips:
   a. Doggie Leg Lift: Kneel on your hands and knees. Lift your right bent knee up to the side, extend that leg out laterally, quickly return to the bent knee position, and back to the floor position. Repeat this action with the left knee. Repeat in succession.

Doggie Leg Lift: Bent Knee Position   **Wall Sit**

Doggie Leg Lift: Extended Leg Position

   b. Wall Sit: Sit against a wall with your feet flat on the floor, your back and shoulders pressed against the wall, and your hands resting on your thighs. Now hold this position for 15-30 seconds, and try to increase to one minute.

3. Arms and Shoulders:
   a. Pushups: With your body supported on your fully extended arms and toes, slowly lower your chest almost to the floor by bending our elbows, and return to the start by straightening your elbows. Keep your back straight and your head up. Do not let your hips or thighs touch the floor. If none or only a few of these pushups can be done properly (they are not easy to do), try to do *negative* pushups: lower your chest to the floor very slowly and then rest momentarily, letting your body touch down to the floor. As quickly as possible, return to the start position *not* by relying on pushing up with the arms, but making it easier by transferring your weight momentarily to your thighs and knees. Now, go back to the starting position and repeat.

Push-Ups: Starting Position

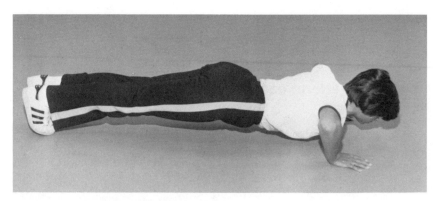

Push-Ups: Lowered Position

b. Arm Circles: Sit comfortably with your arms extended out to your sides. Turn your palms upward and slowly describe small circles with your arms, 10 counts forward and 10 counts backward. Relax and repeat.

Arm Circles—Palms Up

Advanced (Perform each of the following exercises 12-15 times):

1. Abdominals (If these exercises are too difficult, repeat intermediate ones):
   a. Double Leg Lift: Lie on your back supporting yourself up on your elbows. Keeping your lower back in contact with the floor, raise both legs only 10 to 12 inches up off the floor. Then slowly lower your legs to the floor. Repeat

lifting and lowering in succession. Be sure to breathe throughout the exercise and do not arch your lower back!

Double Leg Lift

Trunk Twisting Sit-Ups

b. Trunk Twisting Situps: Sit with your knees bent and your hands clasped behind your neck. Rotate to your left and slowly uncurl backwards towards the floor until your shoulders just touch the floor. Keep in rotation and slowly curl upward to the starting position. Now rotate to your right and repeat the sit-up. Repeat in succession.

2. Legs and Hips:
   a. Combination Side Leg Lifts: Lie on your right side and slowly raise your left leg 8-10 inches and hold. Now raise your right leg to meet the left leg and hold. Then slowly lower both legs to the starting position. Repeat. Roll onto the other side and repeat with the other leg.

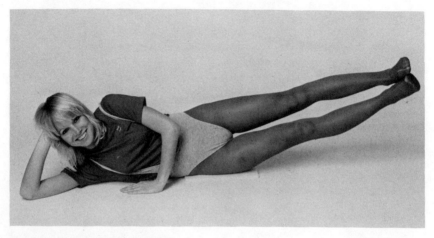

Combination Side Leg Lifts

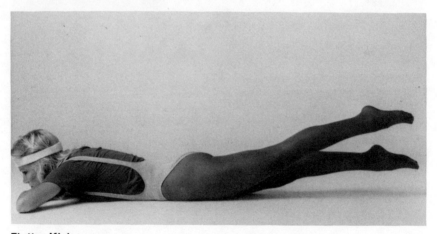

Flutter Kick

   b. Flutter Kick: Lie on your stomach with your head resting on your crossed arms. Lift both legs together up off the floor with your knees straight, and flutter kick 6 counts. Lower to the starting position, relax and repeat. Keep your head down and do not arch your lower back.

c. Seat Walk (this exercise is for overall strength as well as for the legs and hips): Sit with your knees bent and your arms held out to the sides at your shoulders, with elbows bent. Bring your knees toward your chest and "scoot" along the floor by lifting and moving from one side of your buttocks to the other. Keep your feet up off the floor, and use your arms and torso to increase your forward motion. Try to seat walk for several feet. Relax and repeat.

Seat Walk

3. Arms and Shoulders: Repeat Intermediate exercises.

4

Basic Skills in Self-Defense

This chapter covers the personal weapons of the body, vulnerable areas of the body and methods of attack, the basic defensive stance, falling techniques, the ground defense position and finally the four basic steps in self-defense for women.

PERSONAL WEAPONS

If you are attacked, you normally will have to rely on your own body's personal weapons to defend yourself. It is to your advantage to know where these weapons are located and to understand how best to use them. Once you do know how to use these personal weapons, they will in fact be your very best weapons against an attack. I do not recommend that you carry or attempt to use other commercial-type weapons, such as a gun or knife. These are very dangerous weapons, are extremely difficult to learn to use properly, and more importantly can be taken from you and used by the assailant against you! I will even go so far as to issue a caution against the carrying and use of Mace — a chemical sprayed at the eyes and/or groin of the assailant. To be effective, it must be in your hand with your thumb on the nozzle ready to spray at your attacker the moment he grabs you. You will not have time to search through your dresser drawer, the car glove compartment, or the bottom of your purse for your canister of Mace. In addition, women have been shot while trying to ward off a gun attack with their Mace spray—it does have its limits. Finally, it has been found in some of our major cities that repeat offenders have been 'Maced' so often that they are developing an immunity against it! So know your personal weapons and how to use them. They are:

- Head — strike with the forehead or the base of the skull
- Mouth — talk, shout and bite
- Hand strikes — fist, knuckle fist, and fingers (scratch, jab, gouge, pinch)
- Foot kicks — side of the foot, ball of the foot, and heel of the foot.
- Knee — knee-up kick
- Elbow — jab to the rear

Head Strike: Forehead to Assailant's Nose

Head Strike: Base of Skull to Assailant's Nose

Hand Strike: Fist

Foot Kick: Side of Foot

Foot Kick: Ball of Foot

Foot Kick: Heel of Foot

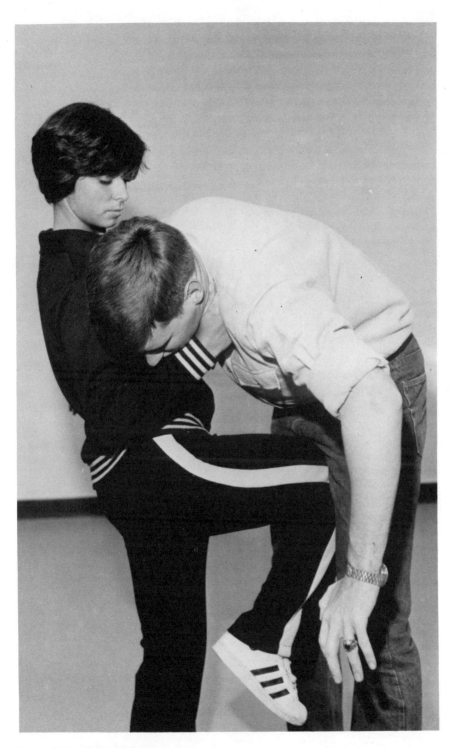

Knee Kick: Knee to Groin

Elbow-Rear Jab to Groin

VULNERABLE AREAS OF THE BODY AND METHODS OF ATTACK

There are certain vulnerable or exposed parts of the body that are particularly susceptible to external blows or pressure and which when attacked properly will cause the assailant a great deal of pain. By attacking these areas, you can lessen the effectiveness of your opponent's hold or attack. Learning how to attack these areas correctly is one of the *most important* elements of any woman's self-defense training. If you remember nothing else but to attack just one of these vulnerable areas in an attack, you have an excellent chance of never becoming another statistic—a victim of rape or some other violent crime.

The skills required to attack vulnerable areas of the body are not difficult to learn, nor do they require a great deal of strength to be effective. Speed and accuracy, however, as opposed to brute strength or size, are essential prerequisites. A few of these self-defense "attack methods" may seem too cruel and vicious to some women. You need to remember that, in most instances, rape is in fact a life-or-death confrontation. Once the decision has been made to react with a counterattack, the effort must be 100 percent with full force. This counterattack may be an attack to one vulnerable area, or a series of blows to many areas. The assailant must be sufficiently hurt or startled to allow the victim time to release herself from a hold, if necessary, and escape to safety. A halfhearted, unsuccessful act of self-defense can easily result in further angering the attacker, who may then try harder to subdue his victim.

A quick reaction or *distraction* is an effort by you to divert the assailant from his assault. Although screaming may be one type of reaction, the primary method of distracting is to commit a painful act on the assailant by attacking one or many of the vulnerable area(s) of his body. Distractions are intended either to cause the assailant to release his hold on you immediately, or startle the assailant momentarily in order to provide you with the additional time needed to complete your release. You will read about the uses of distractions with just about every description of a self-defense release throughout this book.

A retaliation is another response in your arsenal of self-defense actions. *After* a successful release from a hold, and as you are escaping, you may wish to further expand your defense by attacking your assailant's vulnerable area(s) again — a *retaliation*. A retaliation should be a quick attack and should be used to discourage the assailant from attacking or grabbing you again. For example, after a release from a front choke, you deliver a side snap kick to the assailant's knee as you escape or run to safety! However, please understand that you *never* return to retaliate after you are in fact free from the hold. Your objective is to escape your assailant as quickly as possible, not to beat him senseless and leave him in a heap on the ground!

The five most vulnerable areas of the body to attack are: (1) the eyes—any attack to the eyes will cause tearing and blurred vision, and severely gouging the eyes may cause blindness; (2) the nose— hitting the nose will at least cause great discomfort, difficulty in breathing, bleeding or even a broken nose; (3) the throat or neck— striking this area will cause great discomfort, gagging and impaired breathing; (4) the groin—hitting or kicking the groin will cause extreme pain and may bring your attacker immediately to his knees; and (5) the knee or shins—most athletes will agree that the knee is the weakest joint in the body and most susceptible to injury. Any kick to the front, side or back of the knee may cause tremendous pain and immediately halt your attacker. Also, any type of kick to the only slightly padded shin bone(s) will also stop the attacker in his tracks— have you ever bumped your shins on the edge of the bed frame or coffee table? The pain is immediate! If you forget everything else in self-defense, try to remember how to effectively attack at least *one* of these five vulnerable areas of the body.

The following are the best methods of attack to use on the five most vulnerable areas of the body:

- The eyes: Finger jab, thumb gouge or scratch. The eyes are by far the best place to attack your assailant. An effective attack to the eyes can be devastating, and may actually blind your assailant. But remember, you may be fighting for your life. The thumb gouge is the most effective technique to use in attacking the eyes. You grab the attacker's head securely (placing your fingers on the sides of his head to prevent him from pulling away from you), and gouge your thumbs into the inside corners of his eyes. Immediately rake both thumbs across the eyes to the outside corners. This may sound appalling to you, and you know that you would never be able to use this technique. If that is true, then never attempt to use this method of attack. When you attack someone's eyes, you must try to hurt him—just poking the eyes may not hurt your attacker's eyes very much but it will anger him and possibly intensify his attack on you. There are many other types of attacks you may use which may be much better for you as an individual. All I am saying is that this is the *best* attack if you feel you would use it properly. You may actually practice this technique by using a large, round piece of Styrofoam, such as that used for storing a wig. Draw eyes on the Styrofoam and practice grabbing the "head" and gouging the eyes. Keep in mind that this one technique may one day save your life.

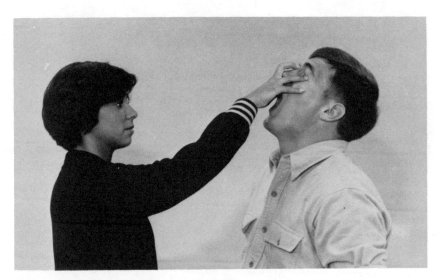

Attack Eyes: Finger Jab

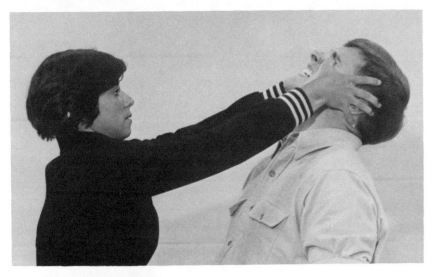

Attack Eyes: Thumb Gouge

- The nose: Palm heel strike underneath, bottom fist strike, double hand grasp strike, and knee-up kick.

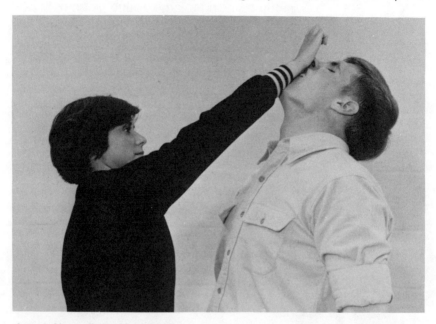

Attack Nose: Palm Heel Strike

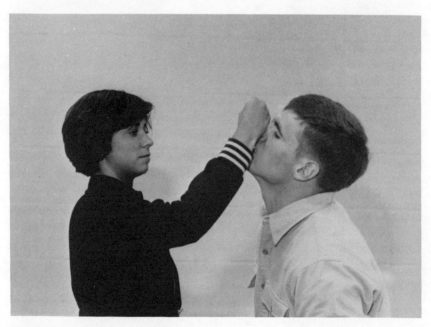

Attack Nose: Bottom Fist Strike

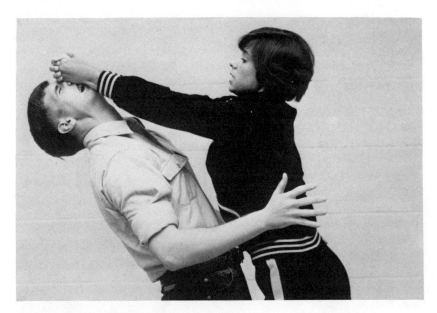

Attack Nose: Double Hand Grasp Strike

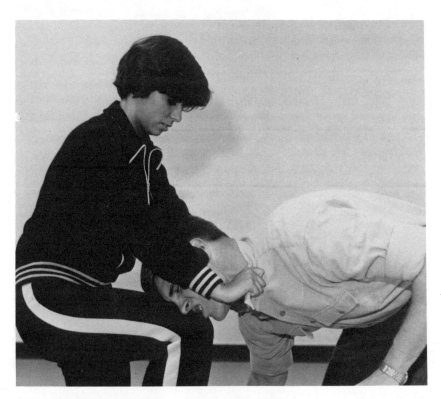

Attack Nose: Knee-up Kick

- The neck or throat: Knife edge hand strike and punch.

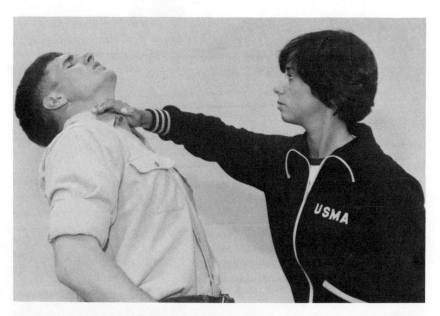

Throat Attack: Knife Edge—Side Hand Strike

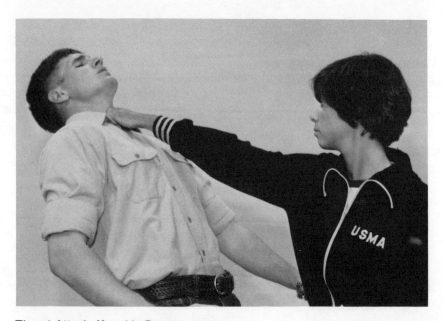

Throat Attack: Knuckle Punch

- The groin: Kick, punch, knife edge hand strike, double hand grasp strike and testicle pull and twist. This last technique may not be done correctly if the assailant is wearing tight clothing. The testicles must be grabbed, pulled and twisted.

Groin Attack: Kick

Groin Attack: Punch

Groin Attack: Knife Edge Hand Strike

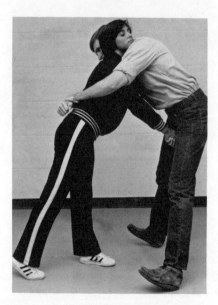

Groin Attack: Double Hand Grasp Strike

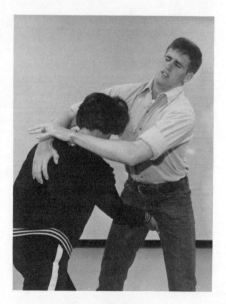

Groin Attack: Testicle Pull and Twist

- The knee
  or shins:

Front, side or rear kick to the knee; kick or scrape the shins.

Knee Attack: Front Kick

Knee Attack: Side Kick

Knee Attack: Rear Kick

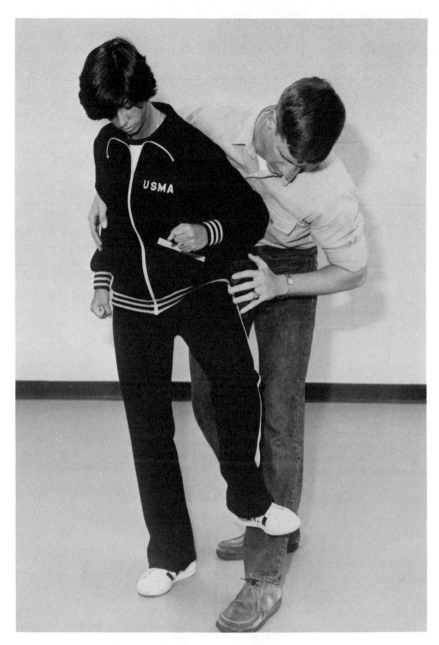

Shin Attack: Shin Scrape

BASIC DEFENSIVE STANCE

For a potential victim, the best position for self-defense is a standing position with your side turned toward the assailant. Once you are on the ground or the attack is from a rearward direction, defending yourself becomes a much more difficult task. As well as providing the best position for self-protection, assuming a good basic defensive stance will demonstrate confidence, authority and aggressiveness— all traits which will discourage your attacker. The defensive stance should protect the most vital parts of the body from attack and enable you to move quickly in any direction—either to escape or counterattack if necessary. The basic defensive stance is as follows:

- The body position:

  The body is turned so either *side* faces the opponent. This position protects the vital organs that are located principally in the front of the body, and also provides a smaller target area to the assailant. Better to be struck on the shoulder than in the chest!

Basic Defense Stance: Right

- The foot position: The feet are approximately shoulder width apart with one slightly behind the other (45-degree angle to the other). The knees are slightly bent; do not lock the knees, as this inhibits movement. The body weight is evenly distributed on both feet so quick movement can be made in any direction.

- The arm and hand position: The hands are held in a closed or slightly open fist. The arm nearer the opponent is held high, away from the body, primarily to protect the face. The elbow is bent and pointing downward, and held in close to the body to protect the ribs. The arm farther from the opponent is held with the elbow bent and lower than the other arm. The hand is in a central position over the solar plexus-stomach area, and moves quickly up or down to protect the face, heart and groin.

Basic Defense Stance: Left

The basic defensive stance may be either a right or a left stance depending upon which foot is forward. Try both stances, so that you will be able to react if you are grabbed from either direction. I find that if you are right-dominant, then generally a right defensive stance with the right foot forward is more comfortable. However, this varies with the individual.

FALLING

Knowing how to fall correctly is very important if you trip during a struggle, or are pushed or thrown to the ground by your attacker. The almost instinctive protective tendency to tense up and put out a hand or foot to break your fall should be avoided. Many unnecessary injuries happen to women who fall in this manner. You have to land safely and be able to return to a standing position as soon as possible.

Once you start falling, you should try to relax and let more than one part of your body absorb the impact of the fall. The best way to do this is to try to roll out of the fall, protecting your head by holding it to one side with the chin tucked to the chest. The roll is generally diagonally across the shoulder and back and should enable you to return to a quick standing position.

Learning to fall correctly may be very difficult for some women. It is important to keep the technique simple, like that for a basic somersault or shoulder roll. Initial practice should be on a mat or other padded surface. It should progress from a stationary squat position to a moving upright position with two or three steps taken before the fall.

Side and rear judo falls are commonly taught in self-defense classes but require quite a bit of skill and practice to perform properly.

Side Judo Fall

Rear Judo Fall

GROUND DEFENSE

If pushed or pulled to the ground and unable to return immediately to a standing position, you should assume a ground defense. This is only held until returning to the basic (standing) defensive stance, which is of course your best fighting position.

Sit with your weight over one side of your body, with the bottom leg slightly bent and the top leg bent and ready to kick. The torso is supported up on one hand, while your free hand is held up by your face. This position will keep the vital areas away from the attacker, and protect your face and front parts of your body. If the attacker moves toward the front vital areas, quickly flip over onto the other

Ground Defense

side, so the buttocks are always toward the attacker. From this position, use kicks at all times to attack and ward off the assailant. Use quick, front and side snap kicks so your foot cannot be grabbed. As soon as possible, slide or scoot back away from the assailant and get up to a standing position. Keep the assailant to your front at all times.

FOUR BASIC STEPS IN SELF-DEFENSE

- *Step One*:   *Avoid* a potentially dangerous situation if at all possible
- *Step Two*:   Attempt to *run* to safety if cover or assistance appears to be near. Do not run just to be chased and then caught while out of breath
- *Step Three*:   Attract attention by *shouting* for help if potential assistance might be near (e.g., shout "Fire!") and
- *Step Four*:   Develop and employ, when necessary, appropriate *self-defense* techniques.

5

Kicks and Kick Defenses

BASIC KICKS: FRONT, SIDE AND BACK

Your legs contain some of the most powerful muscles in the body. As a result, leg kicks are one of a woman's best defensive weapons against a variety of frontal or rear attacks. Leg kicks may be used by women of all ages. Since your legs are longer than your arms, using your legs enables you to put a greater distance between yourself and your opponent than do your hands and arms. Consequently, in most instances, kicking as compared to striking is a much more effective method of self-defense for a woman. The basic kicks described in this chapter are relatively simple techniques that do not require an extraordinary amount of skill or strength to perform. Many of my students have been successful in defending themselves solely by using a quick, well-executed kick to the assailant's shin or knee.

Generally, kicks should be aimed low. Kicks should rarely be aimed above waist level. Kicks to the head may be effective if done properly, but frequently require too much time to learn and perfect. High-flying karate kicks may look good but are not practical for the average woman to use. Also, it is not very easy for an attacker to grab onto a low kicking leg.

The kicks described in this chapter are always best aimed at vulnerable areas of the body—the shin, knee, or at the highest level, the groin. If accurate, they can be painful enough to momentarily stun or startle the opponent. In many instances, a kick, skillfully delivered, can catch an attacker by surprise and enable the victim to escape. It may be the only self-defense skill you will need to use. Be sure to maintain eye contact with the opponent—do not look down at the area to be kicked (this will telegraph the kick). Look the assaulter in the eye and kick him in the knee! In most situations, following the kick, you should be prepared to move away quickly and run from the assailant (unless the initial kick fails, in which case it should be followed by another, better, kick!).

Front kick

The front kick is a fast, short kick used for surprise. The kick is aimed primarily at the shin or knee but may also be directed at the groin, although this is a much more difficult target to kick. The kick starts from the basic defensive stance off of the front foot (either the right or left foot may be the front foot). The body weight is slowly shifted to the rear leg—without making too much movement so that the opponent will not anticipate the kick; then quickly lift the front leg up at the knee (pointing the bent knee at the target). Snap out the leg, kicking with the toe of the shoe or the ball of the foot. Quickly return to the starting position. Be ready to kick again if necessary. Note: Do not kick with the toes unless shoes are worn which will protect the kicking foot.

Front Kick—Starting Position

Front Kick—Finish Position

Front Kick: Rear Leg

The front kick may also be done with the rear leg, which is slower but more powerful. The weight is shifted to the front foot as the rear leg is lifted at the knee and snapped out vigorously.

The front kick as well as the other kicks may easily be practiced at home. Place a firm chair cushion or sofa cushion, or a large, firm pillow up against a wall and kick with full force. The cushion or pillow should be large enough so the area kicked is the approximate height of the shin, knee or groin. If a friend or partner is available to help, the cushion or pillow should be held securely in place. Your partner should be careful to stand to the side, out of the way of the kick.

Practice single kicks as well as multiple kicks in rapid succession. Practice kicking with both your right and left leg.

Front Kick: To the Knee

Front Kick: Practice with a Pillow

Side kicks

The side snap kick is the best kick for you to master. It is a very powerful kick and is aimed at the shin or knee. Since the side of the body is to the opponent throughout the kick, it is a safer skill to use. It can be executed quickly and enables you to escape faster.

The kick is from a basic defensive stance—off your front foot. Shift weight to the rear foot and then lift the knee of your front leg up high so your thigh is parallel to the ground. Shifting your weight backwards is essential in order to get your front leg lifted up high enough, as well as for balance. Quickly kick out sideways with your leg, driving the heel or side of your foot (not the ball of the foot) into the attacker's shin or knee. Return to starting position and be prepared to run or kick again if necessary.

You may practice the side kick with a cushion or pillow just as you practiced the front kick. In addition, any of the kicks may be practiced by standing in a good defensive stance and kicking out repeatedly at an imaginary target. Start slowly and gradually increase speed as you warm up. Be careful not to kick too rapidly or forcefully, since you may strain your knee or hip joint. If possible, practice in front of a mirror so you can check yourself for correct form.

Side Kick: Starting Position   **Side Kick: Finish**

Side Kick: Practice with a Pillow

Side Kick: To the Knee

Back kick

Ideally, you do not want your back to the opponent. However, if an attack is made from the rear and there is not time to turn and face the opponent, the back kick may be used effectively. A back kick is very powerful; it must be executed quickly and almost instinctively, since the attacker is momentarily out of your line of sight.

The back kick starts from the basic defensive stance using the rear leg. Look back over the same shoulder as the kicking leg—looking over the opposite shoulder will twist the body and cause a weak kick. Looking back at the assailant is essential in order to know exactly where he is positioned. Bend forward at the waist for good balance, while lifting the thigh of your kicking leg up into your chest. Vigorously drive your leg straight back into the shin, knee or groin. Strike with the heel of your foot, and at impact your foot should be vertical, with your heel up. Practice with a pillow. Return to the starting position ready to repeat the kick or escape.

Back Kick: Starting Position

Back Kick: Finish

Back Kick: Practice with a Pillow

OTHER KICKS

If your assailant is very close and your body movement is restricted, there are several other kicking techniques that may be used effectively. Any one of these techniques may be sufficient for a release from a hold.

Foot stomp

This kick may be used against either a front or rear attack. Stomp the heel of the sole of the foot down vigorously on top of the instep of the opponent's foot. Repeat if necessary.

Knee-up to the groin

Contrary to popular belief, this kick is not the best kick to use against a male attacker. Generally, men expect this type of attack and are prepared to defend themselves against this kick. However, if done accurately and with surprise, this kick can be most successful in stopping a male attacker. Do not attempt to knee-up to the groin unless you are very close to the opponent, for example, in a front choke or hug hold. Drive the knee-up vigorously into his groin, and if that is not effective, be prepared to do another knee-up, foot stomp or other close-type defensive attack. Be prepared to escape quickly, since if he is not incapacitated, your assailant is most likely to be enraged and may go after you with even more intensity.

Shin-scrape-stomp

This technique is used when the attacker is either to the front or rear. Turn the foot to the side and scrape down his shin, and then stomp vigorously onto the instep of his foot. Repeat if necessary.

BASIC KICK DEFENSE: JUMP BACK AND FOOT BLOCK

Since the kick is relatively easy to use, even the most inexperienced attacker may attempt to kick a victim. It is important for you to be able to react quickly against a kicking attack.

Jump back

The best defense against most types of kicks is to jump back out of the range of the kick as quickly as possible. This defense may be used for almost any kick—slow or fast, high or low!

From a defensive stance with the knees bent, jump back with both legs as the attacker starts the kick (before full leg extension). Put as much distance between you and the attacker as quickly as possible. Be ready to escape or retaliate with a kick if the attacker immediately comes after you again. You may practice alone by jumping back as far as possible from a stationary object—such as a chair set in the middle of a room. If you practice with a partner, have the kicker kick with a front or side kick slowly at first, and react with a jump back. Gradually increase the speed of the kick and jump back.

Kick Defense: Jump Back

Foot block

If in a confined area (i.e., up against a wall) and there is no space and perhaps no time to jump back, a foot block may be used—especially against low kicks to the shin or knee. The block must be done at the beginning of the kick before any full force can be behind it.

From a defensive stance, shift your weight to your rear foot. Now lift the front leg and thrust out the side of the foot at the attacker's shin to stop the kick. Quickly return to the starting position ready to block again or retaliate with a kick.

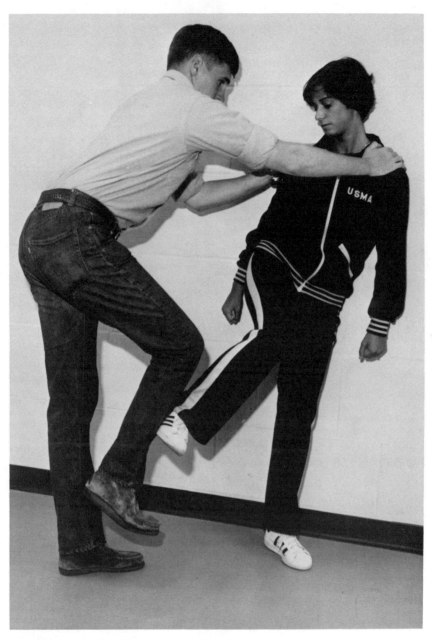

Kick Defense: Foot Block

6

Strikes and Strike Defenses

BASIC STRIKES

Generally, you should not try to defend yourself against a male opponent by using only strikes and punches. Realistically, most women have neither the experience nor the necessary strength and power to get into a fistfight with a man. However, there is a basic punch, as well as several hand techniques, that, if properly practiced and learned, may be used as an integral part of self-defense. This chapter examines these techniques. Strike defenses will also be discussed in this chapter. Any woman who wants to defend herself properly should be prepared to try to ward off a slap or a punch by an assailant. Overcoming the shock of being struck may not be easy for some women. The fact remains, however, that in many attack situations, an assailant will probably attempt to strike or slap his victim.

Strikes, similar to kicks, should always be used against the vulnerable areas of the body. Since your hand is normally not a firm, hard weapon, the bony or muscular areas of an assailant should not be struck (e.g., avoid striking his jaw or chest). Good targets include the eyes, nose, throat and groin. Strikes should be executed quickly, accurately, with full force and with no hesitation or reservations. Angering an opponent with a poorly executed hand technique can easily result in a more determined and violent assault. Be confident. Maintain visual contact with your attacker. Do not look at the area to be struck. If your strike momentarily startles or hurts your assailant, be prepared to run or escape immediately. Do not plan on your punch being so effective that it knocks your assailant unconscious!

BASIC PUNCH

If used properly, the basic punch can be an excellent weapon for a woman. However, thrown incorrectly, the punch can result in an injury to an individual's knuckles, fingers, wrist or elbows.

From a basic defensive stance with the striking hand held in at the side of the body, make a secure fist with the palm up. Having the palm up is somewhat unconventional, but the reason will become clear in the action described below. To make a good fist, curl the fingers into a tight ball and wrap the thumb over the fingers. Do not put the thumb inside the fist or point it upward. A step may be taken with the punch, although it is not necessary.

Basic Punch

Keep the fist tight and the wrist straight. The elbow should drive the fist forward. Just before contact, the wrist is half turned (palm turning inward), and the elbow is straightened. The striking surface is the largest two knuckles. At the same speed and force, the nonstriking arm is pulled in the opposite direction of the punch. This balances the punch and adds strength by putting the shoulder behind the force. Be careful not to throw the shoulders, lead with the elbow or bend the wrist at contact. Immediately withdraw the punch and return to the starting position. Be ready to strike again if necessary. At contact, the victim can shout or yell (e.g., "HIT!") to distract or startle the assailant. In addition, shouting forcefully expels air from the lungs, enabling more force and power to be developed for the punch.

The strike may be practiced from a kneeling position. Punch out slowly, gradually increasing to full speed. This position isolates your hip movement so that your upper body does the work. Change the point of aim: straight forward, upward and downward.

Basic Punch: Practice from Kneeling Position

From a standing position, punch at different speeds in all directions. Throw single right and left punches and then two or three punches in succession. Using an object, lean a chair or sofa cushion against a wall. At arm's distance from the object, punch from a kneeling position. If a partner assists, the cushion may be steadied or held up higher to allow practice from a standing position.

• *Note:* Be sure to practice punching with both the right and the left hand. Generally, the basic punch is easier to throw with the dominant, rather than the nondominant, hand. However, since you do not know from which direction you may be attacked, you must be prepared to strike with either hand.

Basic Punch: Practice Kneeling with a Cushion

Basic Punch: Practice Standing with a Cushion

OTHER HAND TECHNIQUES

Several other hand techniques may be used effectively by women for defending themselves. Since they're generally self-explanatory, only a brief description of them is presented. Many of the same principles for the basic punch are also applied for these other hand techniques.

Pinch and twist Sensitive areas of the attacker's body: ears, nose, lip, inner thigh, groin, testicles, and armpit.

Scratch Especially if your fingernails are long.

Thumb gouge To attack the eyes: Place fingers at side of the head, with thumb in corners of eyes near nose—rake thumbs outward across eyes. This is obviously a gruesome attack which may blind your assailant. However, if your life is being threatened, you must do what is necessary to save it!

Elbow jab If attacked from the rear, strike back hard with bent elbow up to the face (nose, lips or chin), or down to the groin area.

STRIKE DEFENSE

The average male attacker may very probably attempt to strike you. Therefore, it is imperative that you be able to react quickly to protect yourself against these strikes.

Jump back Since a punch is usually thrown quickly, the strike defense must also be fast. Since it is almost instinctive to jump back away from any attempted strike, these actions constitute the best and easiest defense to use. The basic principle here is simply to move out of the line of attack. From a basic defensive stance, jump back as far away from the strike as possible. The front arm is kept up high with the forearm protecting the face and head area. Be ready to retaliate with a side snap kick to the knee, shin or groin while escaping, although if far enough away to escape, by all means, ESCAPE!!!

If alone, practice jumping away from imaginary punches. With a partner, stand arm's distance apart. Start slowly by jumping away from your partner's roundhouse-type punch (the commonly used punch by an assailant). Then have your partner increase the speed of the punch and change to a jab or straight-on type punch without actually making contact. Also, be careful to have your partner aim the punches so you don't get hurt if you move too slowly. Practice defense against both left- and right-hand punches.

Strike Defense: Jump Back

Step back and kick

If the punch is thrown quickly and forcefully, there may not be enough time for you to jump back. In that case, you should try to either step back or shift your body away from the punch. Since you are fairly close to the attacker, this should be immediately followed by a side snap kick to the attacker's groin, knee or shin.

From a basic defensive stance hold one arm up high at all times to protect the head.

As the punch begins, duck the head and shoulders and step back or shift the body away from the attacker. Immediately kick as you continue to retreat. While stepping back may not totally prevent the punch from landing, it should lessen the impact and prevent the assailant from grabbing you.

If alone, practice a step back and kick. With a partner, practice while using slow, roundhouse-type punches.

Strike Defense: Step Back and Kick

Forearm block

Another strike defense that should be only used as a last resort is a double forearm block. If a high, over-the-head-type punch is directed downward at the face or head, and you are either confined or not do not have time to either jump back or step away, the strike may be blocked by the forearm(s). This is dangerous because it will probably result in severe bruising or even breakage of the forearm bones. It is discussed here since it may save you from a serious or fatal blow to the head.

In an effort to protect the bony part of the forearm, the block is made with the muscular or padded part of the arm (with the palms of the hands toward the face). The arms are held up in front of the face close to each other with the elbows nearly touching.

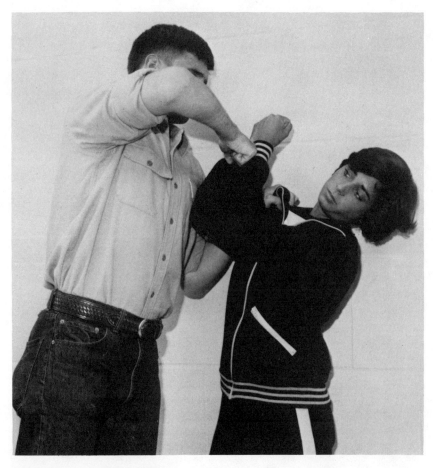

Strike Defense: Forearm Block

7

Defense Against Frontal Attacks

Assailants use many different types of frontal attacks against women. The most common types of frontal holds and attacks are discussed in this chapter: wrist, shoulder, chokes, lapel and hugs. Fortunately, every type of frontal hold and attack can be defended against by a number of techniques. In order to confine a discussion of these techniques to reasonable limits, only the best, most practical and proven defense methods are presented in this chapter. These techniques are easy to learn, and are almost instinctive reactions to frontal attack situations. A self-defense skill that is too complex either to learn, or to master completely, may easily lead to self-defeat rather than self-defense.

You should move as quickly and effectively as possible to escape a frontal attack, no matter how minor it may seem to be. An attack may begin with a simple wrist grab, which, if you do not release immediately, may lead to a much more confining and difficult hold to escape, such as a bear hug.

Most of the defenses and releases for frontal holds include both a distraction and a retaliation. A distraction is used to help loosen an assailant's hold. In some instances, a distraction may also be effective enough by itself to result in your being released. A retaliation is used after the release to discourage the assailant from regrabbing, or again attacking you. Typical distractions and retaliations include kicks and strikes to vulnerable parts of the body. If the distraction and release are successful to the degree that you move safely out of reach of your assailant, a retaliation may not be advisable. You should remember that the primary objective in a situation requiring self-defense is to *escape*, not inflict punishment upon your attacker.

The type of distraction, release and retaliation that should be used depends upon the seriousness of the attack situation. In a very small amount of time, you must decide if your life is being threatened and act accordingly. In reality, the self-defense techniques are dictated by both the attack situation and the defensible skills of the victim. For example, you might use either a knee-up to the groin or an eye gouge on a potential rapist, but would probably not employ similar techniques against a drunk at a party trying to put his arm around your shoulder! Remember self-defense may range from trying to talk an assailant out of the attack to scratching out his eyes.

Practicing the defenses and releases against frontal holds is extremely important. On the other hand, practice is quite different from a real attack situation. In practice with a friend or a partner, no element of surprise exists. The partner holding you knows exactly what you are going to do. In addition, the factor of pain is practically eliminated. It is doubtful, for example, that you will kick your husband or acquaintance in the shins while practicing a wrist release. Consequently, your partner must cooperate to the extent that if a simulated blow looks as though it would cause a release, then he should release the hold. The practice partner also needs to vary the degree of the holds, starting with half-strength and working up to full-strength holds. This should improve both the practice environment and the resultant learning. Another technique that can be employed to improve the practice situation is to increase the element of uncertainty by having the "victim" close her eyes and be attacked by her "assailant." As soon as a hold is applied, her eyes should be opened and the appropriate defense techniques practiced.

WRIST RELEASES

While there are several types of wrist holds, this chapter examines those most commonly used by assailants: single or 1 on 1; double—2 on 1; and 2 on 2. Each wrist hold and the corresponding method(s) of defense for the hold are described. In a majority of the cases, the guidelines are identical for all the wrist releases.

Generally, the wrist hold is one of the easiest frontal holds from which to escape. It is less confining and threatening than most of the other holds. It also leaves several personal weapons free for counterattack.

As soon as the wrist is grabbed, you should initiate your defensive actions immediately, before your assailant can apply his full force to the hold. As a rule, you should not try to *match* your strength against that of a man's. The chances of successfully pulling back and away from an assailant who is holding your wrist is very slight. The techniques presented in this chapter offer a much better defense. At all times, try to stay a safe distance from the holder to prevent him from getting a more secure hold. Keep that arm's distance between you and the attacker, if at all possible.

Single—1 on 1 (front hold over, under or side grip)

This is one of the most common of the wrist holds. An assailant reaches out to grab your wrist and attempts to pull you close to him. It is also one of the easiest to defend against, since only one wrist is being held. Be careful of the opponent's free hand, which may be used as a striking hand.

From a basic defensive stance immediately distract—yell; stomp his instep with your heel; front or side kick the knee or shin. Such actions may be enough to secure your release, but if they are not, take a step around your assailant to pull him off balance momen-

Single Wrist Hold

tarily. At the same time, shoot your elbow up toward him—holding your forearm very close to your upper arm. Turn the wrist being held and pull it up and away over your shoulder. Pull against the thumb and forefingers of the assailant since this is the weakest part of his grip. The release is like a crowbar. Quickly retaliate with a side kick to his knee as you escape.

If alone, practice stepping, the release and the retaliation. With a partner, practice a distraction, release and retaliation. Vary the strength and the type of the hold—right, left, over, under, side, stationary and moving (grab and pull along). Practice with the eyes closed.

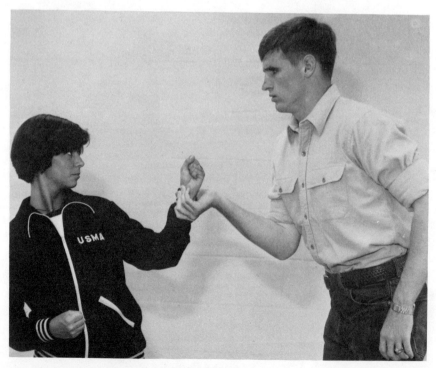

Single Wrist Hold: Close-up of Wrist Twist Out

Single Wrist Hold—Release

Double: 2 on 1

One wrist is held by both of the assailant's hands (over, under, or side grip). This is a more difficult wrist hold to escape since it is more restrictive and involves a more forceful hold by the assailant. However, you have the advantage that one of your hands is free while both of the assailant's are occupied.

From a basic defensive stance, immediately distract to help loosen the hold (see 1 on 1). While stepping around and away from the assailant, reach in with the free hand and grab the top of the hand that is being held; pull it up and away toward your opposite shoulder. (If you pull over the shoulder of the arm being held, you may hit yourself in the face!) Use total body movement to pull free—bend the knees, use the shoulders, and step back all at once. Quickly, retaliate with a side kick and escape.

Double Wrist Hold 2 on 1

Double Wrist Hold 2 on 1: Start Release

Double Wrist Hold 2 on 1: Finish Release Kick

• *Note:* If the wrist cannot be pulled free, continue with distractions and constant movement. A moving victim is harder to hold.

If alone, practice distraction, release and retaliation. With a partner, practice with varying degrees of strength and types of holds—right, left, over, under and side grips. Practice stationary and moving with the eyes opened and closed.

Double: 2 on 2

Both wrists are held in front by the assailant (over or under grip).

While this is difficult to dislodge since it is both confining and forceful, it also places the assailant in a somewhat neutral, awkward position. Since the assailant is using both his hands to hold you, he has to let go of something to assault you further.

From a basic defensive stance, immediately distract to loosen the hold (see 1 on 1). While stepping, momentarily swing the hands outward and then quickly pull them inward, up and away as with the 1 on 1 release. Retaliate with front snap kick and escape.

Double Wrist Hold 2 on 2: Pull arms Outward Momentarily

Double Wrist Hold 2 on 2: Release and Kick

SHOULDER GRAB RELEASES (FRONT AND SIDE)

An assailant may grab onto both shoulders either to shake you, pull you in closer, or throw you to the ground. The defenses for this hold are relatively simple. The release should be done quickly, since this particular hold is usually a prelude to a more dangerous and restrictive-type hold. The defense approach should include a distraction (which may be enough for a release), a release and a retaliation while escaping. Be careful not to be regrabbed.

Shoulder grab release (front)

From a basic defensive stance, quickly distract: yell; stomp instep; shin-scrape and stomp instep; kick the knee or shin; or use a hand strike to the face. Step *back* away and try to dislodge your assailant's hands from off your shoulders with a blow from your fist, swung hard in an arc from the outside in (this is a roundhouse punch). Use total body movement in punching up and across in front of your body. Quickly retaliate and escape, e.g., elbow jab to face, or side kick to knee.

Shoulder Grab: Start Release with Arm Up

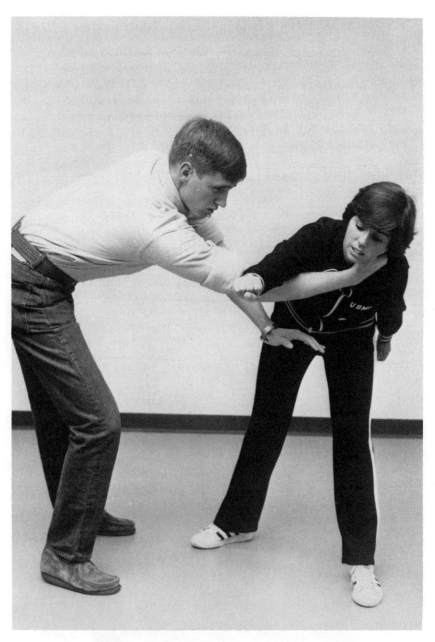

Shoulder Grab: Release with Arm Thrown Across Your Body

Shoulder Grab: Continue Release by Stepping Back

If alone, practice a distraction, the step and punch, and a retaliation. With a partner, practice the distraction, release and retaliation. Have your partner use different degrees of force for the hold. Be careful to avoid actually hitting your partner with either the distraction or the retaliation. Practice with eyes opened and closed. Practice both situations—when you are grabbed only and when you are grabbed and shaken.

Shoulder grab release (side)

This may only be an annoyance-type hold where someone puts an arm around the shoulders. It could also be an attempt to pull you closer for a more confining hold.

From a basic defensive stance, quickly distract: stomp on instep; elbow jab to groin; or turn in slightly and use a hand strike to the face. Aim for groin if it's a serious and threatening attack. If these are insufficient to effect a release, grab one or two of the assailant's fingers at the base and pull back and away. At the same time, step to the outside and behind the opponent. Retaliate as you escape with a side kick to knee.

Practice should be with a partner. Simulate the blows for distraction. Practice the finger pull, being careful not to bend your partner's fingers too far backward. Practice from both left and right sides, stationary and moving (pulling along).

Side Shoulder Hug: Attack the Groin

Side Shoulder or Waist Hug: Release with a Finger Peel

Side Hug: Further Release with a Step Out and Kick

FRONT CHOKE RELEASE

This could be a 1 or 2 hand front choke. A choke is one of the most frightening and serious forms of frontal attacks. If held forcefully for an extended period of time, it may result in impaired breathing, unconsciousness, and even death. Unfortunately, it is frequently used against women.

Defensive actions against a choke should be implemented very quickly. You must not PANIC! Even if free breathing is impaired momentarily, if you employ the proper defensive action, you will have enough time to escape. You should never grab at the hands of your assailant to try to peel his fingers off your throat. This attempt to match your strength with that of your opponent's will most likely be a waste of precious time. Since this is a life-or-death situation, the most serious and injurious types of defenses should be used without any hesitation whatsoever.

Practicing the choke release is essential to proper learning. Certain precautions, however, should be followed while practicing the choke release. When practicing these defenses with a partner, injuries can be avoided by not using a full force choke with the thumbs pressing into the throat. Rather, practice the chokes with the hands either low around the collarbone or with the thumbs along the sides of the neck. Also, just to be safe, have a nonverbal signal for your partner to release the hold if it is painful. For example, tap the floor with the foot twice, or tap the side of your thigh twice or tap the partner's arm twice, etc. The person who is applying the choke hold should be very alert to release the hold immediately if the partner taps out!

Since the choke is a hold applied in close proximity, be sure that the release puts you a safe enough distance from the attacker so that he cannot easily rechoke or regrab you. In addition, your retaliation should be vicious enough that the assailant will be discouraged from continuing his attack against you.

Front Choke Release—1 Hand

With one hand an assailant may grab you by the throat, pushing you back into a corner or up against a wall for further attack. Be careful of the assailant's free hand, which may be used to strike.

From a basic defensive stance, as the assailant grabs at the throat, first try to duck, avoid, and step away. If grabbed, quickly distract: stomp the instep; kick the knee or shin; knee groin; attack the face and gouge the eyes; etc. If not released, quickly step to your side as you do a roundhouse punch across your body. (See the preceding Front Shoulder Grab Release.) Immediately retaliate, if you can do so keeping a safe distance away, while escaping. Throughout the defense, be ready to protect against a strike to your head by the assailant's free hand.

If alone, practice a distraction, the step and punch, and a retaliation. With a partner, practice a distraction, release and retaliation from a right- and left-hand stationary and moving (pushing) choke. Remember to practice the choke hold at the collarbone or with the thumbs along the side of the neck for safety reasons.

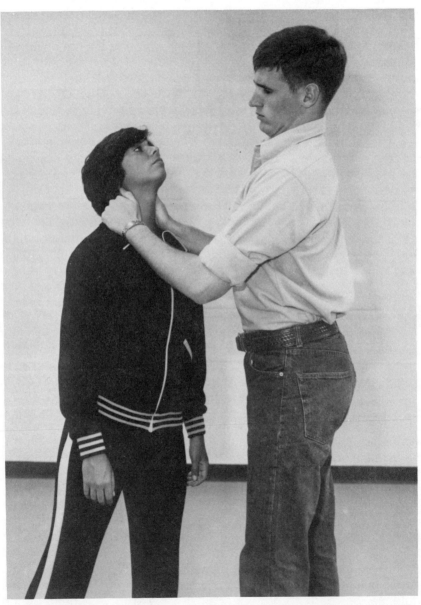

Practice Front Choke: Thumbs on the Sides of the Neck for Safety

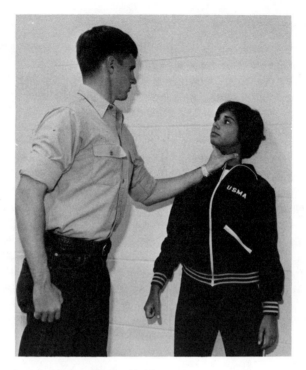

1 Hand Front Choke Hold

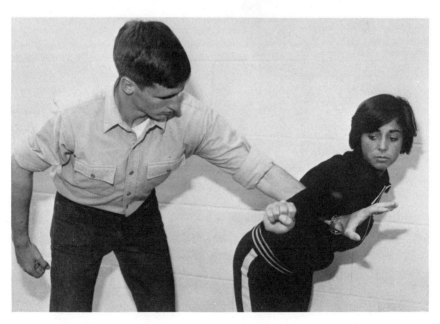

1 Hand Front Choke: Release with Arm Up and Over

Front choke releases—2 hand

This is a much stronger and more dangerous choke hold. The defenses must be immediate, before either panic or unconsciousness occurs. There are several defense techniques for this type of hold, but the best and most successful release is the same one that was described earlier for the front shoulder grab.

From a basic defensive stance, as the assailant grabs at your throat with both hands, first try to duck, avoid and step away. If grabbed and choked, use a quick and painful distraction, e.g., gouge eyes or knee-up to the groin—remember, this is a life or death situation. To release, use the same technique as with the front shoulder grab release, throwing one arm up and over the assailant's hands. Be sure to step as you move your arm. You must put as much body movement into your release as possible. Once free, move away from the attacker as fast as possible—do not be regrabbed!

If working alone, practice a distraction, the release and a retaliation. With a partner, practice a distraction, the release and a retaliation from a stationary choke. Also, practice the choking situation against a wall, both with the eyes opened and closed. Employ safety precautions with this choke. Do not choke with full force!

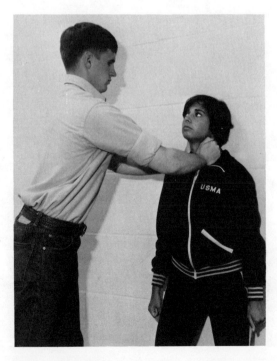

Front Choke Hold—2 Hands

LAPEL OR COLLAR GRAB RELEASE

This may be a single or double lapel or collar grab. The attacker may grab you by the clothing either to pull you in closer or to push you up against a wall for further attack. While this is not an attack commonly used against a woman, it is occasionally employed. The defense should be applied quickly, before a more forceful hold is applied. The best defense is to first try to avoid or step away from the attacker as he reaches to grab the clothing. However, if grabbed, the defensive action should be the same as for a 2 hand front choke release— distract, release and retaliate. The best release is with the step, and throwing your arm up and over.

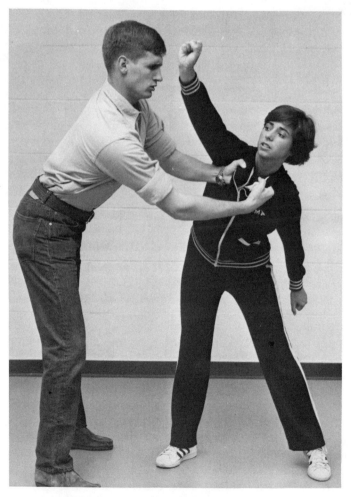

Double Lapel Release—Arm Up and Over

FRONT HUG RELEASES

This may be a body or bear hug from the front, either under or over the arms. Either way, it is one of the most confining and restrictive holds that an opponent can use against a woman from a standing position. It is usually a momentary hold to gain control of the victim, prior to throwing her to the ground for further attack. As such, it is a common attack and an extremely dangerous hold. It should be released as quickly as possible.

There are several distractions or reactions that may be used effectively in succession against a front hug. Because the assailant is very close to you, he has many vulnerable body areas that are open to counterattack. You should select the distractions that work best for you, and use them. Also, as long as the front hug is being held, the assailant cannot attack further. In most instances, this will permit you more time to counterattack and hopefully escape.

As soon as the hug is applied, place your feet shoulder width apart, bend your knees and lower your center of gravity. This makes you a more difficult object to control, lift up and throw down to the ground. If there is a chance of your losing your balance and falling, try not to fall backwards where the assailant can land on top of you on the ground. Lean forward and try to fall, landing on top of the opponent—a position from which it is easier to defend yourself.

Since the hug is an extremely close attack, be sure that the release puts you a safe distance from your attacker. Discourage further attack by using serious and painful types of distractions and retaliations.

Front Hug Release—Over the Arms

A front hug where the arms are pinned to the sides of the body is the most common type of front hug.

From a basic defensive stance, as the attacker reaches to hug, first try to avoid or step away. If grabbed, quickly distract using three or four attacks in succession: yell; stomp the instep; shin-scrape and stomp the instep; kick the knee or shin; knee-up to the groin; clasp the hands together if possible and punch the groin; or butt your forehead to his face. Try to create space so the hold is not so confining. If the distractions do not result in a release, try jumping downward and back away as your arms are lifted upward—like an umbrella. This should knock the opponent's arms off your shoulders and upper arms. If necessary, use your hands to help push his arms off of you. Immediately retaliate as you escape, and then move a safe distance from the opponent.

The jump may be practiced as described above. With a partner, practice a series of distractions, the release and a retaliation. Although the distractions should not be applied full force, the hold should be released once it appears as if the distractions would be effective. Practice with different degrees of force in holding, both with the eyes opened and closed. Practice both stationary and moving.

Front Hug Over Arms: Create Space with a Groin Hit

Front Hug Over Arms Release: Jump Down and Back

Front Release—Under the Arms

A front hug where both of your arms are free is an easier hug from which to escape because your hands and arms may be used in your release. Although in most instances the attacker would usually not grab under the arms, it may happen. It may also be that the attacker did a front hug over the arms and you were able to pull one or both arms free but were still being held.

From a basic defensive stance, try first to avoid or step away, but, if grabbed, use any three or four of the following distractions, as quickly as possible: yell; attack the eyes; pinch and twist the lip; strike the nose or throat; knee the groin; or kick and scrape the shins and stomp the instep. Remember your hands are free, so any combination of these attacks should result in a release. Retaliate, while escaping, and move a safe distance from the assailant.

8

Defense Against Attacks from the Rear

Although there are several types of attacks from the rear that may be used against a woman, only those most frequently used by assailants are discussed in this chapter: wrist, chokes, hugs, and the 1 arm hammerlock. The defensive techniques and releases presented for each rear hold are simple, practical and proven.

Any kind of attack from the rear is a highly dangerous and frightening type of hold. Most attacks from the rear are a complete surprise to you, which makes defending against these attacks more difficult. The reaction to the attack must be immediate. In short, the defense techniques must be so well known by you that they are virtually instinctive. Any delay in the self-defense reaction may mean the difference between life and death.

Distractions and retaliations are a very important part of the defenses against attacks from the rear. In most instances, quick and accurate counterattacks to the assailant's vulnerable areas can enable you to secure your release. These counters should usually be a series of three to four simultaneous blows. Since the chances are that you will not see your assailant, any attack from the rear should be, as a general rule, treated as an extremely dangerous and life-threatening act or assault and your counters should be forceful ones.

Similar to the frontal attack defenses, practicing the defenses for the attack from the rear is vital if you want to learn the proper techniques and be able to execute these techniques quickly and accurately. Partners need to cooperate and to observe safety precautions at all times. Be very careful while practicing the rear chokes. Full force should not be used while practicing these holds. In addition, simulated counterattacks should be used, rather than making actual contact. In order to simulate more closely the surprise element of an attack from the rear, the "defender" should close her eyes while practicing her defensive reactions and techniques.

REAR WRIST RELEASE—2 ON 2

One type of assault from the rear occurs when both wrists are grabbed from behind and held by an assailant. His grip may be either overhand or underhand. The aim of his attack may be to control the victim, to pull her closer to him or to pull her to the ground for further attack. Although this hold places you in a somewhat awkward position, it is easier to escape from it than from a more confining hold, such as the rear hug. Consequently, the release can be quick. You should be careful to stay a safe distance from the attacker once you are released. A common error made while trying to escape from this hold is to attempt to step forward and pull the arms straight out of the hold. This is usually a waste of time and energy since the assailant is frequently stronger than the victim.

Rear Wrist Hold 2 on 2: Start Release With Step Back

From a basic defensive stance with your back to the attacker, as soon as the wrists are grabbed, distract to the rear: yell; back kick to the knee or shin; stomp the instep; or scrape the shin and then stomp the instep. Momentarily step back toward the attacker with your knees bent and your body leaning forward; then quickly step forward with the elbows bent in close to the sides of your body, and pull the wrists forward, up and away as with a single wrist release. Retaliate with a side snap kick to the knee while escaping. Do not step back toward the attacker to kick him. Kick only from a safe distance while you are stepping away.

If alone, practice the step back and the distraction, then the forward release. Timing is important. With a partner, practice the distraction, release and retaliation. Vary the degree of force in applying the hold. Practice with the eyes both opened and closed. Practice with both a stationary and moving hold.

**Rear Wrist Hold, 2 on 2: Finish Release with Step
Forward and Wrist Pull Forward**

REAR CHOKE RELEASES

This may be a 1 hand, 2 hand or forearm choke from behind. As with front chokes, the possibility of impaired breathing, unconsciousness and even death exists with any of these rear chokes. Unfortunately these very dangerous holds are frequently used in assaults on women. They must be reacted to with speed and efficiency. It is no time to panic! In these life-or-death-type holds, use only the most vicious distractions and retaliations. Practice is essential, but be careful that full force while choking is not used. Simulate your counterattack while observing all safety precautions. Employ the same "modified" choke and "tap-out" method as was used to practice frontal chokes in Chapter 7.

1 hand over mouth release

This hold is typically used by an assailant to keep his victim quiet while he attempts to gain control for a more serious type of attack. In this type of hold, one hand usually covers the victim's mouth very tightly while the other grabs her arm or upper body, pulling her closer to the assailant. Since your breathing may be impaired, you must secure a release quickly.

From a basic defensive stance with your back to the attacker, distract immediately: try to bite the hand; yell; back kick to the knee or shin; stomp the instep; elbow jab the solar plexus; or punch the groin. If still held, reach up and grab 1 or 2 fingers (little finger is often the weakest) and pull back and away. Step off to the side of the attacker while pulling at his fingers. Retaliate with a side snap kick to the side of the knee as escaping. Be sure to stay a safe distance from the assailant once released.

Practice must be with a partner. Practice a distraction, the release and retaliation. Be careful that the partner's finger is not pulled too far back. Grab from both sides of the defender. Practice with the eyes both opened and closed. Practice both stationary and moving holds.

Rear choke release—two hands

On this choke, the assailant has both his hands firmly around the neck of his victim from behind the victim. It is a very strong and frightening hold. Impaired breathing and unconsciousness may result within seconds. The release must begin the absolute second the choke is applied.

On this hold, the distraction is optional. You may want to go immediately into the release. If, however, the release is not totally effective, then distractions should be used immediately. (See preceding 1 Hand Over Mouth Release.) To release, quickly throw

Rear Hand Over Mouth Hold: Release with Finger Peel

one arm up, stepping slightly forward and turning around to face the attacker. Turn in the same direction as the arm that is raised. The turn should knock the assailant's hands off the throat. Immediately retaliate with a strike down to the attacker's face or clavicle as you back away. Keep a safe distance from the assailant to avoid being choked again. Remember, as stepping away, the side of your body and not your back should be to the attacker. Do not turn your back on the attacker too quickly once you attempt to escape.

If alone, practice the arm-up-and-turn and a retaliation. With a partner, practice all steps with your eyes both opened and closed. Do not use full force in choking. Follow all rules of safety. Practice only a stationary hold.

Two Hand Rear Choke: Release With Arm Up and Turn

Rear forearm choke release

This choke is applied from behind the victim with a forearm held firmly across her throat. The hold is usually the most dangerous of the choke holds because it is both strong and very confining. Unconsciousness may result within seconds. As soon as breathing is impaired, you may get some relief by turning your head into the crook of the attacker's elbow. The release should then follow. There is a possibility that you may either see or sense the attacker's arm as it comes around from behind. If this is the case, you might be able to duck and step away in time to avoid the choke.

Rear Forearm Choke: Turn into Crook of Elbow for Relief

If not, distract immediately to try to loosen the hold and create some space in which to move: yell; back kick the shin or knee; punch or elbow the groin; bite the arm; butt the head backwards to the attacker's head; or stomp the instep. Now to release, use a counter joint action: Place the palm of one hand under the attacker's wrist, with the fingers curling up under his lower arm, and the palm of the other hand under his elbow joint. Simultaneously pull down on the wrist and jerk up on the elbow, creating a space. Turn the head inward and step back, slipping down and out through the open space. Be sure to step out backwards—do not turn around to face the attacker. Quickly retaliate, such as with a side snap kick to the side of the knee while escaping. If, when trying to back out, the attacker gets your head into a headlock, viciously attack the groin, jab the eyes, stomp the instep, etc.. until the release is completed.

Rear Forearm Choke: Distract with an Attack to the Groin

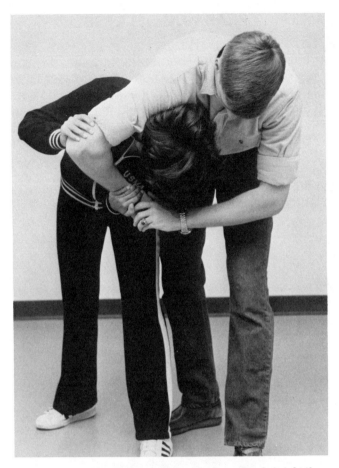

Rear Forearm Choke: Release with Counter Joint Action

- *Note:* Another release for this hold is a shoulder throw. It is not discussed in this text because throws generally are more difficult to learn, and they are not as practical as the aforementioned technique. Unfortunately, for a throw to work the assailant must be in a perfect throwing position—which is most likely not going to happen in a street attack. It looks very good on TV, but throws are just not for the average women. In addition, in order to practice the throws, a partner must be willing to be thrown and must know how to fall correctly in order to avoid possible injury.

The counter joint action must be practiced with a partner. Practice the releases initially in slow motion and then at a faster rate in order to achieve a realistic practice situation. Practice all safety precautions, especially the nonverbal "tap-out." Vary the force of the holds, and choke from both sides of the victim. Practice with the eyes both opened and closed, and from a stationary as well as moving position.

REAR HUG RELEASE

You may be held in a rear hug, over or under your arms. This is a more common type of hug attack then the front hugs. It is a confining, forceful hold. The rear hug may be applied by an assailant to control his victim, lift her up and throw her to the ground. Defenses should be quick and forceful. Since this type of hold may lead to a much more serious attack (e.g., rape), the distractions and retaliations should be extremely vicious. To be most effective, the distractions should be in a series of three or four as was described for defense against front hugs (Chapter 7, end). When grabbed, quickly try to bend the knees and lower the center of gravity. This should make it more difficult for the assailant to pick you up and throw you to the ground.

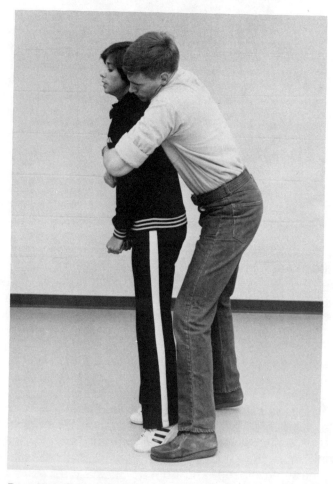

Rear Hug Over Arms Hold

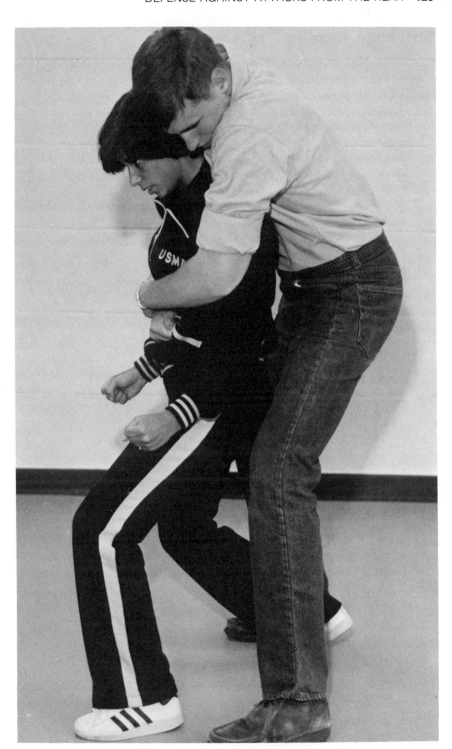

Rear Hug Over Arms—Start Release by Lowering Center of Gravity

Rear hug release—over the arms

This type of rear hug occurs when the victim's arms are held tightly and are pinned to the sides of her body. This is the most common and dangerous type of rear hug attack.

As the attacker starts to grab you, try to step away and avoid before he can fully apply the hug. If grabbed, quickly distract, using three or four attacks in succession: e.g., yell; create space by moving the hips to one side and attacking the groin; kick back to the knee or shin; scrape the shin and stomp the instep; or butt the head back to

Rear Hug Over Arms—Move Hips to Side and Hit Groin

the face. If still being held, try to grab one or two fingers and peel backwards while stepping away. If the hug is applied high on your arms, try to jump down and away as the arms are lifted abruptly upward. Retaliate after any of these releases with a side kick to the knee while escaping. Get a safe distance from the assailant to avoid being regrabbed.

Rear Hug Over Arms—Release with Finger Peel

Rear Hug Over Arms—Release by Jumping Down and Out

Rear Hug Over Arms—If Lifted Up, Hook Leg

• *Note:* If an attacker grabs you and lifts you off the ground, try to hook his ankle or leg as he lifts you up. Continue with distractions. A moving and fighting victim is much harder to hold!

Practice with a partner the distractions and each of the releases. Simulate blows and have the holder release accordingly. Vary the force of the hugs. Practice with the eyes both opened and closed, from a stationary and a moving hold. Also practice with the victim being lifted up.

Rear hug—Under the arms

This is a rear hug where both of the victim's arms are free. It is not as frequently used by assailants as the rear hug over the arms. It should be easier to escape from, since the arms, hands, and legs are free to counterattack.

As the attacker starts to hug you, try to avoid his hold. If grabbed, quickly execute three or four distractions in rapid succession: e.g., yell: reach back to grab his hair and pull his head forward to gouge his eyes; kick back to the shin or knee; shin-scrape and stomp the instep; butt the head back to the face; or elbow jab back to the solar plexus

Rear Hug Under Arms—Grab Hair and Jab Eyes

and up to the face. If still held, knuckle punch the back of the hand, grab one or two fingers, peel back, and step out and away. Once released, retaliate with a side kick to the knee as you escape.

Practice with a partner. Practice a series of distractions, the finger peel and retaliation. Vary the force of the hold, practice with the eyes both opened and closed, and from a stationary and moving hug. Also practice the lift up.

Rear Hug Under Arms—Release with Finger Peel

1 ARM HAMMERLOCK RELEASE

One arm is bent and pushed up the back. Your arm is usually held by the assailant at your wrist and elbow to reinforce his hold and prevent your escape. This may be used as a come-along hold to move you to another place. It is not a very secure hold and usually not too painful because most women have a wide range of flexibility in the shoulder joint. Also, the other arm and the legs are free to use in counterattacking.

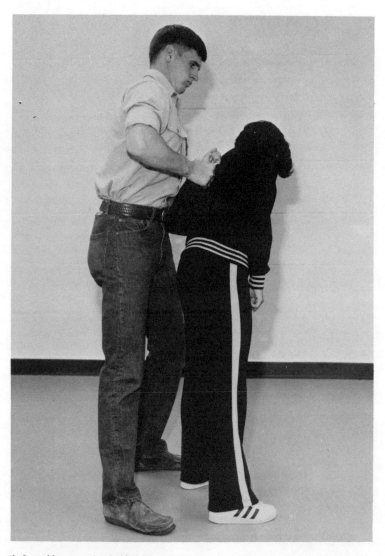

1 Arm Hammerlock Hold

To release, distract to the rear: e.g., with the free arm, strike the groin; elbow jab back to the solar plexus or up to the face; back kick to the knee or shin; or do a shin-scrape-stomp to the instep. If still held, step off to the side of the attacker, pulling your held arm straight out while stepping. Step to the same side as the arm being held. Execute a single wrist release (Chapter 7) if your wrist is still held. Quickly retaliate with a side snap kick to the side of the knee while you escape.

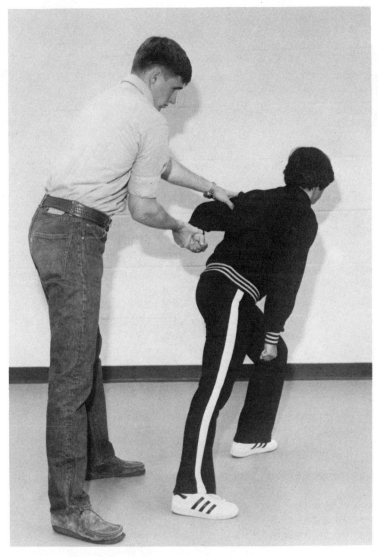

1 Arm Hammerlock—Start Release by Stepping out

1 Arm Hammerlock—Finish with a Wrist Release

You should practice with a partner. Practice a distraction, the release and retaliation. Vary the force of the hold. Grab from both sides of the defender. Practice with the eyes both opened and closed, and from a stationary and moving hold.

9

Defense Against a Weapon

Always cooperate with an armed assailant. If his motive is robbery, give up your valuables. A general rule is never resist if a weapon is held directly to your body. However, as soon as the weapon is away from the body—react quickly and viciously. Remember, an armed assailant may only be using a weapon to threaten or frighten you into doing what he wants. As much as possible do as he says and save your life!

Since the possibility always exists that the armed assailant will attempt to kill his victim after robbing or assaulting her, defenses against weapon attacks should be learned. These should only be used as a *last resort*, as in a life-or-death situation. Weapon defenses presented in this chapter are for use against the most frequently carried weapons: a club, knife and pistol.

CLUB

A club can take many forms: a piece of wood, a lead pipe, a baseball bat, a broom handle, etc. The most typical types of club attacks are striking from an overhead position downward toward the head; and striking from a sideward position, hitting the neck or side of the body in the area of the kidneys or ribs. The defense is as follows: Be in a basic defensive stance. This is very important because it places the side of your body to the attacker. This will give him fewer vulnerable areas to strike. As soon as the strike begins, jump back as far as possible off both feet. One arm should be held up to protect the head. Try to hold the head off to one side for further protection. Quickly retaliate with a side snap kick to the knee or shin while escaping. Do not step back into the range of the club to kick your assailant. Keep a safe distance from his weapon.

Overhead Club Attack

Overhead Club Attack—Jump Back

- *Note* It is not recommended that you try to block the club attack with your forearms. This could result in serious injury. However, if you are in a confined space where jumping back is impossible, a last resort would be to protect the head with the arms as in the basic forearm block already presented in Chapter 6.

Practice must be with a partner. Use a plastic bat such as a Wiffle bat, or a cardboard tube, e.g., the insert from a roll of wrapping paper. Practice swinging the club from both overhead and sideways. Start with a slow swing and gradually increase to a more realistic type of attack. Practice the jump back and kick. Timing is most important.

How to use a club

If the assailant drops the club or you happen in any way to gain possession of his weapon, use it with care. Do not swing the club. Hold it firmly in both hands and jab forward at vulnerable parts of the assailant's body, e.g., eyes, throat or groin.

How to Use the Club Against the Assailant

KNIFE

If at all possible, stay a safe distance from an attacker who has a knife. To use it, he must be close to you. If you are grabbed and the knife is held directly to your body, do not resist or move a muscle! Remain calm and try to talk to the assailant. Watch to see if the knife is put aside, and then react! If the attack is an overhead or sideward thrust to your body, you have an opportunity to defend yourself. This is an instance where some defense is better than none, since you

Overhead Knife Attack

probably will be seriously injured if you do nothing. Although you should expect to be cut while defending against a knife, being cut on the arm or leg is much better than being cut on the head or face area. Probably your only opportunity for defense will occur on the initial thrust. Be alert and quick to escape. Try to wrap a piece of clothing around one arm to aid in the defense. For an overhead or sideward knife thrust, the defense is as follows: Be in a basic defensive stance with your side to the attacker. As soon as the knife thrust begins, step back with the covered forearm held up to protect the head. As soon as possible, attempt to put as much space between you and the knife as is necessary for your safety. If the knife is slashed at you from the side, redirect or parry the hand holding the knife. Immediately retaliate with a side kick to the shin or knee while you escape. Also, be careful to keep a safe distance from the knife by using the kick. If the assailant grabs onto you and thrusts with the knife, quickly pivot or turn away and immediately attack his eyes or groin. There will not be time to step back.

Overhead Knife Attack—Step Back

Slashing Knife Attack—Parry

• *Note:* Use any available object to help keep the knife away. Strike or block with a chair, table, piece of wood, or throw dirt into the eyes of the attacker. If by chance the attacker drops the knife, do not attempt to use it. Either retain it while you escape or throw it far away.

Practice must be with a partner. Use a rubber knife, a sturdy, rolled-up piece of paper, or a small cardboard tube to practice. Thrust from both an overhead and sideward direction. Start slowly and increase to a more realistic speed.

PISTOL

As a general rule, if a pistol is aimed at you, do nothing! Remain calm and very slowly try to talk to the assailant. Ask what he wants and comply with his every wish since death may be a very strong possibility. Any slight movement could cause the attacker to fire his weapon. Do *not* yell for help.

If a "pro" aims a pistol at you, the weapon will rarely be against your body or within your arm's reach. He will place the pistol back near his hip and stay away from the reach of the victim. If robbery is

Pistol Attack

the motive and the victim cooperates, the professional probably will not shoot his victim. He knows that the police typically search harder for a murderer than for a robber. On the other hand, the amateur with a pistol will probably be nervous and as likely to shoot as not.

Although there are defensive techniques which may be used against a frontal or rear pistol attack, they are difficult to master and will not be discussed here. The best defense against a pistol is to cooperate; do nothing until the weapon is put aside. If you get the pistol away from the attacker, do not attempt to use it. Take it with you as you escape or throw it far away from the reach of the attacker.

Out of fear, many women have begun to keep small handguns in their purses for self-protection. Generally, I do not believe that this is a good practice. If you should have the opportunity to pull your gun out against a potential attacker, do you know whether you would be able to shoot that person? Would you hesitate long enough for him to disarm you? Would an unarmed assailant quickly become an armed assailant? Do you know how to fire a pistol safely and accurately? Would you miss your target and anger your assailant even more? There are just too many unknowns for the average woman to try to defend herself with a pistol.

10

Defense Against Two or More Assailants

Most assaults against women involve only one assailant. Statistics, however, indicate that there are a few gang-type attacks on women. Also, some professional thieves work in pairs. Fortunately, they normally are only seeking valuables and are not intent on harming their victims. In some situations, however, a woman is forced to defend herself against two or more assailants. Although her chances for escape are fewer, she should follow a number of defensive principles if she is attacked in this fashion.

In the first place, a woman alone should never be walking in a neighborhood where youth gangs hang out. If approached by such a gang, she should remain calm. In most instances, the group may try to frighten her with intimidating catcalls or obscene language, but will probably not attack. If possible, the woman should ignore the comments and continue walking. If stopped, she should speak with the group. This should be done calmly and rationally. She should not show fear. As much as possible, she should demonstrate complete confidence.

If by chance a gang consisting of three or more does decide to attack her, he should—for safety reasons—cooperate with their demands. Defending against so many assailants is extremely dangerous and almost impossible. The woman can save her life by *not* resisting in this type of attack situation.

The following are defense techniques that can be used against two or more assailants:

2 Against 1—One in Front and Other with Rear Hug, Kick Front Attack First and Then Release Hug

2 Against 1—Both Holding Wrist, Kick One First

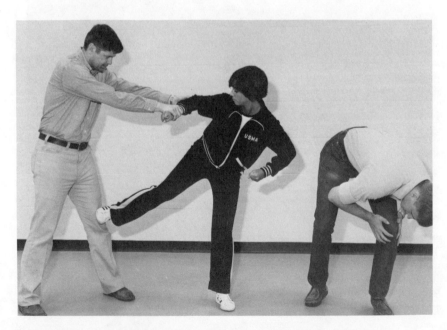

2 Against 1—Both Holding Wrist, Kick Other Attacker Second

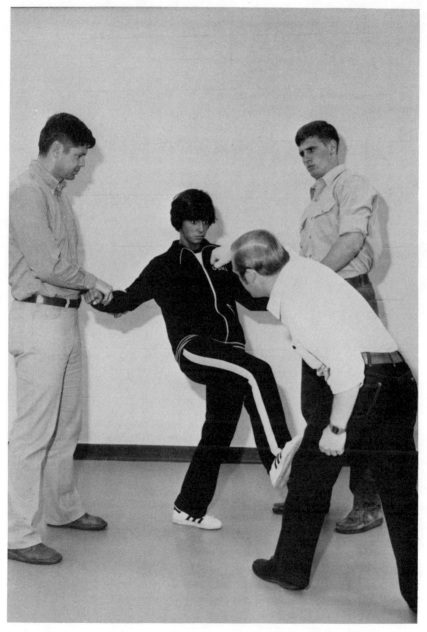

3 Against 1—2 Holding Wrists and 1 in Front About to Hit, Kick to Front Person First

1. If a weapon is used, try to cooperate with the demands of the attackers.
2. Try not to let one of the attackers get behind you. Move to keep both assailants in front of you.
3. Defend against only one assailant at a time. Do not get in the middle of the two attackers so that they can assault you simultaneously. Try to stand closer to one of the assailants to pressure him to attack first. Assume a defensive stance, deliver a quick side snap kick to the knee or shin of the one attacker, then immediately turn to the other and kick. Quickly escape.
4. If in a populated area and attacked simultaneously by two assailants, do as in the aforementioned and yell "Fire!".
5. With two assailants, do not try to look directly at both at the same time. This would cause one's head to be constantly turning. Observe both of them by using peripheral vision.
6. In a situation with two assailants, if one grabs you with a rear attack and the other approaches you from the front, first deliver a front snap kick to the knee, shin or groin of the attacker in front; and then quickly try to escape the rear attack. Do not try to defend against both attackers at the same time. Eliminate the one to the front of you first.
7. In a situation where two assailants are each holding one of your wrists from the sides, execute a single wrist release first from one side and then from the other. Do not try to escape both at the same time. Try to escape the less forceful hold first. Remember that a moving and kicking victim is much more difficult to assault.
8. If held by two assailants, with each holding one of your wrists, and a third individual approaches you from the front and attempts to grab or strike you, defend against the oncoming assailant with a front snap kick. Follow with the wrist releases (Chapter 7) and several kicks while escaping as in number 7, above.

11

Rape Defense

Hopefully, the safety measures and self-defense techniques discussed in previous chapters are sufficient to prevent a rape from actually occurring. Rape, however, is a grim reality in our society. According to numerous sources, it is the fastest growing violent crime in the United States. The statistics regarding rapes are startling, especially with the consideration that at least half the rapes that are alleged to occur are not reported.

Rape is a crime in which a woman is forced to perform a sex act without giving her consent. It is a crime of violence, not sex. It is often performed to degrade, dehumanize and brutalize the woman just because she is a woman. Women who have been rape victims often suffer emotionally for months and even years after the actual attack.

Unfortunately, there are many myths associated with the crime of rape:

1. That rape victims provoke their attackers by acting or dressing seductively. This is pure fabrication. A rape victim may be any age, may be very unattractive, and may be dressed in almost anything. What seems to be important to the rapist is that the victim be female, available and vulnerable;
2. That the victim enjoys and actually wants to be raped. On the contrary, most rape victims abhor the violence of the rape attack, and are in constant fear for their lives throughout the act;
3. That the woman could have resisted the rapist more forcefully. Most victims resist the rapist as much as is physically and emotionally possible;

4. That a rapist is a real "stud" and "he-man." This is untrue; the typical rapist is insecure about his masculinity and may in fact be raping a woman to gain power;
5. That all men are potential rapists. On the contrary, a normal, healthy male seeks sexual gratification from a woman, while a rapist seeks something entirely different; and,
6. That the "typical" rapist is older, rather seedy-looking, has a knife or gun, and is a stranger who attacks his victim on dark street corners. The "typical" rapist is usually in his teens, of average appearance, generally does not carry a weapon, and in nearly half the reported cases rapes his victim in her home.

Whether or not to resist a rape attempt is an individual question. Every woman should decide now if and how she should resist a rapist. It must be remembered that with rape the possibility of severe, even fatal, bodily harm exists. More and more rapists are murdering their victims to eliminate witnesses. One woman may decide that her life is the most important thing to her and cooperate with the rapist. She had rather submit than be brutally beaten. Another may feel that

Whether or not a woman should resist a rape attempt is an individual question.

the trauma of being raped would be so severe that she had rather take her chances and resist. Studies have found that any pre-thought at all about how to prevent or to deal with an actual rape will help you much more if it happens than if you absolutely refuse to believe that "it can happen to me."

There are several verbal and physical techniques that may be used to defend against rape. There is no one *best* method to resist rape. Each of you must decide which technique is best for you. The following are some examples of how to defend against rape:

1. Do not panic. Remain calm and try to talk the rapist out of the assault. Many women have been successful in talking their way out of a rape attack. Tell him that you are menstruating or pregnant, or that you have VD, cancer or some other terminal illness. Try to get the sympathy of the rapist, or at least distract him.

2. Delay and stall for time. You may tell the rapist that you are ill and make yourself vomit, or that you must go to the bathroom first. Complain of menstrual cramps; many men are often ambivalent about this condition. Suggest having either a drink or a meal first. Suggest going someplace more comfortable. As a rule, never go to his place or yours. Any of these techniques may give you some time to better plan out what you are going to do, and may even cause the rapist to change his mind about the sexual assault.

3. Try to disgust the rapist by putting your finger down your throat to induce vomiting; pick your nose, urinate or defecate on the spot. Any of these actions may change the mind of the attacker!

4. If the rapist has a weapon, such as a knife or a pistol, it is probably best to do as he says. Your life is in danger and resisting would more than likely be futile. If by chance the weapon is put aside, then resistance again becomes a possibility. Remember, is is not easy for the rapist to undress you, undress himself, have intercourse—all while holding a pistol to your head. Try to be aware of the location of the weapon.

5. If you decide to resist and there is a possibility that help is near, yell "Fire" to attract attention. Do not yell out if there is a weapon or if you are in a completely deserted area, because the rapist might be frightened enough by the noise to attempt to silence you even more forcefully.

6. If you feel that your life is in danger, and that you will resist no matter what, you should act quickly and viciously. Commit yourself completely to your own self-defense. Attack the most vulnerable areas of the assailant—the eyes, throat,

nose, groin and knees. Show no mercy! Attack forcefully and be prepared to escape as soon as the rapist is momentarily injured, stunned or distracted. If possible, severely hurt and disable the rapist—do not just anger him. You are likely to have the advantage of the element of surprise since the rapist will not expect you to take up the attack yourself. He selected you as a victim because he thought he could overpower you, and that you were vulnerable. Prove him wrong!

7. You may pretend to cooperate, and when the rapist is preoccupied, and his guard is down, attack violently and viciously.

8. As soon as you are thrown to the ground or the floor, the ground defense should be assumed and the defenses begun. This may prevent the rape assault from proceeding further, especially if you are successful in delivering a quick and forceful kick to his groin.

9. Never remove your own clothing; make the rapist do this. His hands will be momentarily occupied, which will make him more vulnerable to attack. The rapist is also vulnerable when he removes his own clothing.

10. Situation: The potential rapist is sitting on top of the victim undressing her. *Action:* Gouge his eyes, quickly get your feet under your hips and lift up, simultaneously throwing one

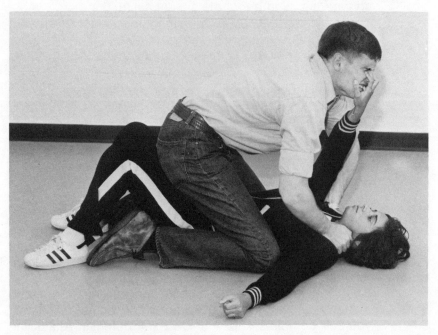

Defense Against Rape: Eye Gouge

Defense Against Rape: Hip Up and Leg Over

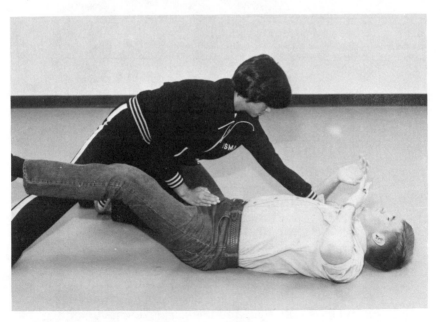

Defense Against Rape: As Escaping, Attack Groin

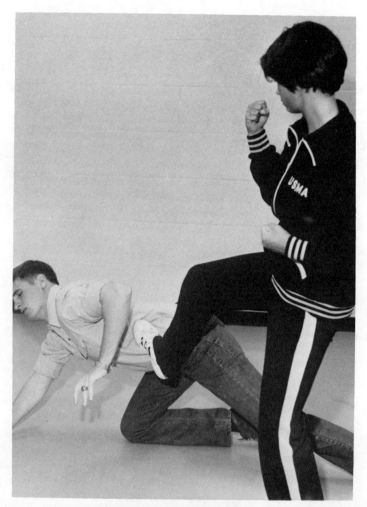

Defense Against Rape: Kick the Attacker As He Starts to Get Up to Re-grab you.

leg over to one side. Push the rapist at the shoulders in the same direction. Follow up with an attack to the groin, stand up as soon as possible and escape. Be sure that the eye attack is severe enough to allow time for the release. Also be sure to be ready to kick or attack the rapist again if he starts to get up to re-grab you. Then escape. Note: This "hip-up and leg-over" technique is one of the few methods I have found that can actually get a 200-lb. man off a 120-lb. woman. We have practiced this skill often in our co-ed self-defense classes and it does work. Women have very strong hips and legs, and this skill takes advantage of that physiological fact.

If you are raped, there are several things that must be done:

1. Report the crime to the police immediately. Do not wait one hour or until the next day. Reporting the rape is essential and may prevent the rapist from assaulting someone else. Too many rapes go unreported because of the embarrassment and shame felt by the victim, as well as the fear that the rapist may someday return if the attack is reported.

2. Do not wash or douche yourself, or change, wash or destroy any clothing worn at the time of the attack. This is often difficult for the rape victim. She feels very dirty after the rape and her first impulse is to shower or bathe, which of course will destroy valuable evidence against the rapist.

3. Get medical attention immediately. This should include both a medical and an internal examination, for your own protection as well as to obtain evidence of the crime. You may have been injured or given a venereal disease, or may even be pregnant as a result of the rape. Point out bruises, scratches or any other injuries to your body. These may be photographed and used as evidence later in court.

4. As soon as you are able, you should be ready to inform the police of all the details of the rape attack—no matter how intimate. You should also try to give as complete a description of the assailant as possible: height, weight, age, color of hair and eyes, clothing; automobile if used, weapon if used, and anything else unusual that might help to identify the rapist. If you feel that you cannot face this ordeal, or reporting or even discussing the rape alone, there are professionals available to assist you. Throughout the United States, there are rape crisis centers with counselors (often on call 24 hours a day) who will help you with every aspect of this reporting procedure. I have spoken with many rape victims who have praised the work of the people at these centers!

5. More often than not a woman will need help in coping with the trauma of the rape experience. This help must start at home with an understanding husband, boyfriend, children, friend or relative. In addition, outside professional help may also be required. This is not unusual. In fact, in most instances the rape victim *should* seek out professional counseling and advice. After rape, some women never again feel safe, no matter how carefully they live their lives. The fear of again becoming a victim is overwhelming. Individuals who have training to assist rape victims include chaplains, priests and rabbis, mental hygienists, psychologists and counselors. Also, as I mentioned previously, several major cities in the U.S. have rape crisis centers, which offer valuable assistance to the rape victims.

6. Finally, there has been widespread improvement in the way rape victims in the U.S. are now treated by the police, courts and hospitals. Laws in most states have been toughened, conviction rates for rapists are going up and judges seem to be more likely to give more stringent sentences to offenders than ever before. There is hope for the rape victim!

12

On the Town: Using Public Places and Public Transportation Safely

With the increase in the number of women working outside the home as well as an increase in the amount of travelling they must do alone, several safety precautions and preventive measures exist that these women should take in certain situations. Unfortunately, crimes and assaults involving women occur anywhere, at any time. Women should avoid potential dangers, no matter where they may arise, and should at all times be alert to their surroundings.

Specific locations where a woman out alone could easily be attacked need definite safeguards. These areas are: public places such as a restaurant or bar, a motel or hotel, an elevator, an airport, a theater or a place to recreate—a gym, pool, sauna, park, etc. and on public transportation such as a bus, train or subway, or in a taxi.

If you fail to heed the safety precautions and preventive measures presented in this chapter, and an assault on you is attempted, the self-defense techniques discussed in previous chapters will be required. Remember, you should never be embarrassed about defending yourself in a public place. Attract as much attention and assistance as possible, and do whatever may be necessary to protect yourself!

The following precautions should be taken when you are using public places:

Restaurant or Bar

1. Go to reputable, well-patronized, well-known restaurants and bars. If alone, avoid an out-of-the-way place, even if the food is supposed to be the best in town.
2. Avoid swinging singles places when alone.
3. Avoid sitting in dark areas of the restaurant or bar. Try to face the entranceway and have most of the room in full view. Generally, do not put your back to the door.
4. If alone, sit near the cashier, at the counter or at the bar, where assistance is available if needed.
5. If at night, be sure to park your car close to the restaurant or bar, or take public transportation that stops directly at the front door.
6. Do not accept an offer from someone you just met to be walked to your car or escorted home. Also, do not accompany someone with whom you just have become acquainted to his home.
7. Notice if anyone follows you as you leave. If suspicious of someone, immediately return to the establishment and inform the manager.
8. If alone, do not accept food or drinks from someone you just met. Generally, it is better to go "dutch treat" for awhile.
9. If annoyed by someone verbally or physically, leave him and tell the manager. At times, speaking out in a loud voice, "leave me alone" will be enough to get rid of annoyance. Do not be afraid of making a scene.
10. If alone, be careful of how much personal information you give out to a stranger. Even if you meet an interesting man and desire to meet him again, you first name only and a phone number should be sufficient information. He will call if he is geniunely interested.
11. You should know your liquor capacity and not exceed it if alone in public. Alcohol dulls the senses and limits your ability to protect yourself!

Motel or Hotel

1. Stay at a well-known and reputable motel or hotel, even if it is slightly more expensive or a little out of your way.
2. Be sure all windows and doors in the room are well secured. The door to your room should have a door chain and more than one lock. When you first walk into your room, check all the doors and windows. If you are not staisfied with the security, ask for another room. Avoid ground floor rooms, which are more easily accessible to burglars and peeping toms. I once checked into a hotel in

When traveling, you should stay at a well-known and reputable motel or hotel, even if it is slightly more expensive or a little out of your way.

a major city and was given a room with a sliding glass door leading out to the pool area. I tried the door, found it open and discovered that someone had taped the lock to the open position. I called security and they found 5 other unlocked doors on my floor—apparently set up to be burglarized.

3. Upon entering your room, do not hesitae to look under the bed, in the closet, behind the shower curtain or out on the balcony. Unfortunately, I have had a couple of students who have found intruders in their hotel rooms—one in a closet and one on the balcony. If you do in fact find someone in the room and he does not have a weapon, scream for help, throw things and generally make as great a commotion as possible.

4. Check to see if a switchboard clerk or desk clerk is on duty all night. This may be someone you can reach in case of an emergency.

5. Register using your last name and only the initial of your first name. This will help to prevent anyone from knowing that you are a woman staying alone.

6. Leave your valuables in the hotel safe if one is available. If your valuables must be left in the room, hide and secure them as much as possible—locking them in your suitcase is not sufficient!

7. Do not leave your luggage unattended in a hotel lobby, hallway or somewhere by the front desk. If necessary, check it with a bellboy for safe keeping; they usually have a locked closet for temporary storage.

8. Answer the door to your room with caution, and use the door chain or peephole to see who is at the door (this includes someone who is supposed to be room service or the maid). If you do order room service (which many women do who travel alone), leave the door open while you sign for your order and the food is put inside your room. Be suspicious of hotel 'repairmen' who come to your room to fix something you did not report as broken. Check with the desk clerk first—it is possible that a previous occupant reported a need for repairs.

9. When leaving your room, even for a short trip to get ice, close and lock your door. It is also a good idea to leave a radio or television playing to discourage intruders while you are gone.

10. Be careful not to be followed by someone when going to your room. If you suspect someone, quickly return to the lobby. Do not let the person see which room is yours.

11. Have your key unobtrusively out and ready to open the

door. Do not stand in the hallway searching through your purse for a room key.

12. When you stay in a motel or hotel, use the staff's expertise about the city you are visiting. Ask them for directions, schedules of public transportation, typical cab fares and for place to eat and shop which are within safe walking distance of the hotel.

13. You do not need to stop your recreation or physical activity program because you are away from home.

Many of the large hotels now have indoor recreational facilities: pools; gyms; weight rooms; a running track; saunas; etc. Check on the hours of operation and try to avoid those hours that the facilities may be deserted. But you may not even need to leave the hotel in order to recreate.

If you are a walker or jogger, check with the hotel staff for recommendations about safe routes to use. Tell them approximately the time and distance you want to go. Be sure the route is easy to follow, and that you would not be completely isolated if you did get lost. In general, avoid parks, running trails or par-courses. These may be more appealing as a jogger, but they are not as safe for women alone. Avoid exercising outside in the very early hours or late evening hours. Try a lunchtime run or take a late-afternoon break from meetings to run. No matter what time you choose for your outdoor activity, carry a whistle to get assistance if you need it—yelling for help while out of breath is very difficult!

If you are away from home and exercising outside, be sure to wear or carry some type of identification. If you should become a victim of a mugging, assault or rape, you want the police to be able to identify you. This is also true of joggers who are running near their homes!

Elevator

1. Do not step onto an elevator if a suspicious-looking person is already in it. Wait for the next car.

2. Before entering the elevator, check to be sure in which direction it is going. Do not spend any extra time on the elevator riding in the wrong direction.

3. Upon entering the elevator, try to stand near the control panel. Push the alarm button to get assistance if necessary. If someone suspicious get on, the buttons for several different floors may also be punched so that the door opens frequently.

4. Another reason for standing near the control panel on the elevator would be to prevent someone else from turning out the lights or using the emergency stop. Believe it or not, women have been raped on elevators that had been stopped between floors.

5. Do not leave the elevator if a suspicious-looking person is lingering in the hallway. Ride to another floor and exit there, or return to the lobby.

6. If the elevator is crowded or too slow, do not take the fire stairs. These should be used for emergencies only.

Theater

1. If at night, be sure to park your car close to the theater in a well-lighted parking lot. If taking public transportation, get off as close to the entrance of the theater as possible. Also, be sure you know the safest and quickest route to the theater from your transportation.

2. If alone, sit in an aisle seat or close to a family.

3. Keep your purse and any other valuables on your lap, not on the seat next to you.

4. If you are annoyed by someone (verbally or physically), immediately leave and tell the theater manager or an usher. Do not talk to the person or react to him in any way. Just get up and leave!

5. Try to avoid going to theaters alone, especially at night, in unsavory neighborhoods—even if the most popular show in town is playing there. Try going to the matinee; it will probably be safer for you.

6. When leaving a theater, check to see that no one is following you. If you are followed, immediately return to the theater and get help.

Airport

1. If you are travelling alone, try not to schedule flights which would put you in an airport in the early morning or late evening hours. A crowded airport is generally safer.

2. If you are driving to and from the airport alone (especially in unsafe hours), try to park as close to the terminal as possible. It may cost more but it probably will be safer than parking in "long term" parking areas.

3. If you are alone and need to park and leave your car, drop your luggage off and check it at the curb. You do not want to be slowed down with your luggage while you walk from the parking area to the terminal, and you should always have your hands as free as possible.

4. Be careful that you are not followed while walking to and from your car and the terminal. If you are, try to return to the safety of the terminal or your locked car, whichever is closer.

5. Be sure that you have sufficient gas in your car to get you to and from the airport. Your return trip may get you into the airport when gas stations are no longer open.

6. Upon arriving in a city where you have never been, check with the Traveler's Assistance desk. They can advise you on the availability of public transportation to your hotel or any other destination you may have, on the approximate cost of such travel, how much time it should require, and on the best routes to take. If the Traveler's Aid desk is closed, one of the car rental clerks will usually answer your questions. This advice is for reasons of economy as well as safety: A few years ago, I attended a convention alone and took a cab from the airport to the convention hotel. Unfortunately, I did not find out how much the trip usually cost and paid twice the amount my fellow-conventioneers paid! By overpaying I gave the impression of not only being dumb but also of being vulnerable. I now try to stay in hotels that have transportation to and from the airport.

The following precautions should be taken when you are using public transportation:

Bus, Train Subway or Taxi

1. If traveling alone, try not to use public transportation—especially at night.

2. Know the time schedules for the different modes of public transportation. This should help you avoid a long wait.

3. If you are waiting for transportation, stand in a well-populated and well-lighted area. Avoid deserted bus stops, subway stations and platforms. If very few people are around, check to see if you can stand by a manned refreshment stand or change booth, or wait in a nearby store or cafe.

4. Always have the proper change ready when the transportation arrives. Do not display more money than is absolutely necessary. Use a separate change purse.

5. While waiting for transportation, be alert at all times. Never fall asleep while waiting for or riding on public transportation.

6. Sit near a driver, conductor or motorman. Try to find an aisle seat from which you can quickly exit if necessary.

Taxi drivers in large cities are generally trustworthy. Do not hesitate to ask the driver to wait until you are safely inside a building before he leaves.

7. Try to sit in a car on a train or subway with other passengers. If almost everyone exits, move to another car that has more people, or to a position next to the driver.
8. Always carry the proper change to make a phone call in the event you become stranded.
9. Hold your purse and packages. Do not put them on the seat next to you.
10. If annoyed verbally or physically, leave immediately and tell someone. Do not talk to the person or react in any way if possible. Just leave.
11. If travelling alone at night, try to arrange to be met by someone at your point of exit.
12. While exiting from a vehicle, check to see if someone seems to be following you. If you are followed, return to the vehicle if possible. Otherwise, seek assistance at a residence or a place of business. Do not lead the potential assailant to your home.

13. If you are riding in a taxi, check to see that the picture of the operator matches the driver. Also note the driver's name and identification number. Try not to let the driver know if you are a complete stranger in his town—you may end up going for a much longer and more expensive ride than necessary.

14. Taxi drivers in large cities, however, are generally trustworthy. Do not hesitate to ask the driver to wait until you are safely inside a building before he leaves.

15. If you are going to need a taxi at night, call for one or go to a nearby hotel or restaurant where cabs may already be waiting. Do not expect to find a taxi immediately, especially in bad weather.

13

Self-Defense for Specific Individuals: Senior Citizens, Children, the Battered Woman, and the Couple

Certain groups of females are especially vulnerable to attack and should take extra precautionary measures in order to defend themselves. Senior citizens, children, "battered women," and members of couples account for an extraordinarily high percentage of female victims of assault, and they should be even more concerned about their personal safety than the average woman.

THE SENIOR CITIZEN

Unfortunately, a would-be rapist is interested in all women by virtue of their sex alone, regardless of their ages or appearances. The senior citizen, especially in the big cities, is becoming a larger and larger part of the crime statistics involving women. However, just because a woman is elderly does not mean that she is incapable of defending herself. On the contrary, many of the self-defense techniques presented in preceding chapters can be used successfully by the senior citizens. A few years ago I received a letter from a "senior" woman in Columbus, Ohio. She had heard me talking about self-defense on the radio one morning. A few days later she was putting out her trash in the garage underneath her apartment, and someone grabbed her by the trash bin. She remembered what I had said about yelling "Fire," which she did. She so startled her assailant that he ran out of the garage without harming her. In addition, her yells brought help, and pursuers even caught the assailant. Now, that is self-defense at its very best!

In addition to the preventive measures already discussed in Chapter 2, there are other safety precautions that the senior citizen *in particular* should follow:

1. Ensure that your residence is secure, that multiple locks are on all the doors and that all windows are locked.

2. Try to live in a safe neighborhood where the neighbors are relatively near-by. Know your neighbors. Work out a plan for helping one another in an emergency. There is usually safety in numbers. If you do not already have a "Neighborhood Watch Program," call the local police to discuss such a program. You seniors can have the most efficient Neighborhood Watch Program possible, because many of you are at home at all hours of the day and night.

3. When going out, try to go with a friend, or better yet with several friends. If at all possible, avoid performing errands alone, especially if you are walking at night.

4. Do not carry valuables or large amounts of cash on you. When shopping, carry only what is necessary. Put your money in different areas: small coin purse, inside and outside pockets, shoes, etc.

5. Do not display money in public. Keep all your money transactions as private and discreet as possible.

6. Do not establish a set routine to do daily errands. Vary the time and the place both for shopping and outings—including when you walk your dog!

7. Beware of purse snatchers and pickpockets. Carry a small, obscure purse that has zippers and several compartments—and if possible, do not carry a purse at all. Put your valuables elsewhere. If an assailant demands your purse or valuables, do not hesitate to give them to him. Your life is more important than your valuables! If an assailant approaches and indicates that he wants your purse, hand it to him or drop it in his direction before he grabs for it and knocks you down in the process—so many senior women have been injured in this type of purse-snatching. Do not have anything on you that you would hesitate to give to a mugger if necessary.

8. If you are home alone, have a light or radio on in another part of the house to give the appearance that someone else is home with you.

9. When actually leaving the house even for a very brief errand, such as putting out the trash, getting the mail or picking up the newspaper, lock the door. It only takes a second for an intruder to enter your home.

10. Have a dog as a pet. Your pet does not have to be a trained "killer" dog. In many instances, even a small dog's bark discourages a potential prowler or attacker.

11. When out in public, be alert. Check periodically to see if you are being followed. This is especially important when returning from the bank or the Social Security office. If someone is following you, immediately go to a residence or place of business for help. Do not lead the person back to your home.

12. Have your retirement checks, Social Security or other monthly checks sent directly to your bank rather to your home. This will prevent their being stolen out of your mailbox, and keep you from making regular trips to the bank with checks.

13. If your keys are lost or stolen, change the house locks immediately.

14. Be smart about where you hide any valuables at home. It is best to keep cash and jewelry in a bank or safety deposit box. However, if you must keep valuables at home, hide them well. Senior's homes are favorite targets for burglars—they expect you to have cash around the house!

15. Beware of home improvement contractors who come to your house uninvited. They may offer you a price to do repairs that is "just too good to be true." More than likely they have no intention of doing any repairs, and are just trying to get a better look at your house to burglarize it. If repairs are in fact done, they probably will not be done very well. If in doubt, check with the local Better Business Bureau or your local police department. If the contractors are legitimate, they will be licensed, bonded and registered.

16. Be concerned about personal safety at all times. Do not be careless. Have confidence in your ability to prevent a crime before it happens.

CHILDREN

Among the most distressing sex crimes are those involving a child. These may include a wide range of acts, from indecent exposure and abnormal sex acts to actual sexual intercourse. The effect upon the child is often deeply injurious, both physically and mentally. The trauma of this type of assault take years to overcome.

It is the responsibility of parents and adults to educate children so that the possibility of assaults against them can be decreased and hopefully eliminated altogether. It is important that children understand that their attacker may be not only a stranger but someone he/she knows, a family friend, a relative or a casual acquaintance. Crimes against children should be prevented before they occur. The following are specific preventive measures for children:

1. A child should not take money, food or other gifts from a stranger. Children should also tell their parents or another adult if such an offer even occurs.
2. A child should not accept a ride from a stranger even one claiming to have been sent by the child's parent.
3. Be sure that a child knows his/her name, address and phone number. This is essential information if the child is lost or found somewhere injured. Establish a procedure for your child to follow if he/she is lost, i.e., tell a salesperson, a policeman, etc.
4. Teach a child to use the phone in an emergency. Have the phone numbers of the police, fire department, and place of your business or employment next to the phone in a highly visible place. At very least, be sure your child knows how to dial "O" for operator asistance.
5. Know where your child is going, and with whom. Get to know the child's friends and their parents. Encourage your child to bring friends to your house.
6. A child should not be out at night alone, and should avoid playing near empty or isolated areas. A child should not cut through alleys, vacant lots, or take other shortcuts coming home, especially at night.
7. When children are walking alone, they should try to act as strong and confident as possible. They should be alert and aware of their surroundings at all times. If they think some-one is following them, they should cross the street, change direction, run or go into a store or business for assistance. The child should not go home if no one is home. Each child should have someone's home to go to in an emergency, where an adult will be home.
8. If alone, a child should not enter the home of a stranger or even a casual acquaintance. Many of the cases of child-molesting are perpetrated by someone the child knows slightly.
9. He/she should never invite a stranger or casual acquain-tance into the home. If your child is alone, explain to the child that no information should be given on the phone or at the door to a stranger. Also be sure that your child tells you if such a request is made by a stranger.
10. Your child should be taught not to allow anyone—friend or relative—to touch or caress intimate parts of his/her body. if this should happen, the child should report it to you imme-diately. Teach your child to respect the body.
11. Tell your child to inform you if someone indecently exposes himself.
12. You should select baby-sitters with great care. Get recom-

mendations from your close friends or neighbors, and try to get to know the baby-sitter yourself before leaving your child alone with anyone.

13. Teach your child to understand that it is not his/her fault if someone does bother or hurt him/her. Emphasize how important it is that you be told about the incident—no matter how frightened or guilty the child may feel.

14. More and more self-defense classes are being taught to children. Check with your local schools and police department(s) to see if such programs are being offered.

15. With proper instruction, your child can learn the importance of being careful, but not develop an intense fear of all strangers.

THE BATTERED WOMAN

The problem of the "battered wife or woman"—a woman beaten or abused by her husband or boyfriend—is a national problem, which no longer should be regarded as merely a "domestic squabble." Although wife-beating is a violent crime, it is one of the least reported. Numerous women are beaten repeatedly, many to the extent that they require medical attention, but still they often do nothing about it. Some women fear being beaten again. Perhaps a greater fear is that their taking action will result in a divorce and their having to support themselves and possibly their children. Consequently, the battered woman tells herself that it will never happen again, or that she provoked the beating in the first place.

There are a number of things a battered woman should do to help herself:

1. You should never allow your husband or boyfriend to hit or beat you more than once. Do not believe your husband if he claims that it was an accident and will never happen again. Statistics strongly indicate that it probably will occur again, and again, and again!

2. Encourage your husband or boyfriend to get professional assistance or therapy. Help him to understand that he has a serious problem.

3. You should not blame yourself for being beaten or feel guilty that perhaps you provoked the beating. However, if your husband or boyfriend is known to lose his temper easily, and you must in fact live with this, try to remain calm when he is yelling or is visibly upset. This may avoid a confrontation in the first place.

4. If you are afraid that your husband or boyfriend will hit you again, leave the house at once. Go to a neighbor, or to a shelter for battered women. Seek counseling, legal action or whatever else is necessary. Do not wait around for the next beating!

5. If you have been assaulted by your husband or boyfriend, you should call the police and file a complaint. This is especially true if children are involved. Do not wait until the next time to get assistance, because the next time it happens, he may kill you or harm your children.

6. You should seek help if you are a battered woman. There are many possibilities for you. You are not alone. Wife-beating no longer needs to be a private matter! Telephone hot lines have been established in several cities all over the United States to provide advice for the battered woman. Shelters are being established to get women and their children out of the home and away from the husband or boyfriend. Check with local churches and/or YWCA's to find out if such shelters exist in your community. Rape crisis centers and women's centers of many types may also be of assistance to you. Remember, you need not incur an assault more than once, or suffer in silence!

THE COUPLE

Every couple should decide ahead of time what they will do if attacked. There are times when a husband is seriously injured because he refuses to let his wife give up her jewelry or other valuables to a robber. I had a student whose husband was shot because he refused to let her give her wedding ring to a mugger on the street. Luckily, he was not seriously injured and she was able to explain to him that he meant much more to her than her diamond ring.

Decide before going out for the evening what you would do in a robbery or assault attempt. If you know you will not be out in the best part of town, do not overdress, and leave your cash and good jewelry at home. Generally, if the assailant has a weapon—and most of those who attack couples do—it is best to give up your valuables without hesitation. In the event that no weapon is used in the attack, then the couple can work together using the self-defense techniques presented in this book to ward off the attacker.

14

Recognizing Potential Assailants

Individuals who attack women have different characteristics and mannerisms. You should be able to quickly recognize the most common types of potential assailants. Not all potential attackers are seedy-looking middle-aged characters who lurk on dark street corners. A young, attractive businessman type dressed in an expensive three-piece suit may also be a potential assailant. Nor does the attacker have to be a man! Many of our large cities have statistics on women muggers also. In fact, one of my students related her experience in New York City. She was coming out of a large department store around noon when a young woman came up to her on the crowded sidewalk, put a knife at her stomach and demanded her money. She was so startled, she quickly gave her money to the girl and stood "frozen in her tracks" for several minutes after the mugger left. So, beware—your attacker could be a woman!

The following are traits that should be recognized as typical of some kinds of potential assailants:

1. A professional thief will most likely carry a weapon. His main interest is normally in your valuables. If they are relinquished quickly enough, you will probably not be harmed. In addition, the "pro" knows the consequences of being caught and the severity of committing murder. Be cooperative, however, because he knows how to use his weapon and if provoked, will. There is controversy about whether or not to make eye contact with a professional mugger. Some police officers say to make eye contact because it shows that you are not as easily intimidated. Others say not to look directly at the mugger because he may think that you will be able to identify him more accurately later.

2. The amateur thief with a weapon may be much more dangerous. He is probably nervous and fearful. Any resistance on your part could trigger him to use his weapon. In many instances he is under the effects of either drugs or alcohol and probably is not rational. With this type of assailant, be very careful. Be calm and cooperative. Do not make any quick moves or gestures. Stay a safe distance from him if possible.

3. A "panhandler" or "street bum" typically wants any handout he can get. He probably does not carry a weapon. In most instances, he is harmless. In general, ignore this type of assailant and keep walking.

4. Be suspicious of strangers on the street. In some instances, however, an individual who needs assistance may legitimately approach you—for example, to ask for directions. If it does not require you to subject yourself to any personal danger, you should help him. If alone, however, it is probably best to speak as little as possible and refer him to someone or to somewhere else for help. Occasionally, a potential attacker may test his victim by trying to talk to her first. So keep this in mind on the streets and do not be overly friendly or cooperative.

5. The comon traits of a "typical rapist" are:

   - He is most typically in his teens, unmarried, unskilled, of low intelligence, has a low income and is unsure of his masculinity.

   - Most rapes are planned. In at least half of the reported rape assaults, the victim knew the assailant, who may be a casual acquaintance, a date, a neighbor, a coworker or a friend of a friend.

   - Most rapes occur in the warmer months, on a Saturday, and between 8 PM and 2 AM.

   - Most rapes occur in the victim's own neighborhood, when she is alone and in isolated surroundings.

   - Most rapes are not committed for sex but to degrade and dehumanize the woman. Many rapists have hateful and very aggressive feelings about women. Psychologists state that rapists want to "put women in their place."

   - In short, an individual often becomes a rape victim merely by being (for her) in the *wrong* place at the *wrong* time!

15

Self-Confidence: The Key to Survival

Preventive and precautionary measures, rape awareness information and the most commonly needed self-defense skills and techniques have all been presented in *Self-Defense for Women*. After reading this book you now possess sound information about personal safety. The next step is to actually apply the preventive measures and to learn the defensive skills. Preventive measures are easy enough. Defensive skills depend entirely upon the *individual*. Perhaps the ultimate question that must be answered by all women contemplating how they can and will act should they be assaulted is: Do I possess confidence in my ability to defend myself? In most such cases, self-confidence is the *key to survival*.

Building self-confidence is best accomplished through both mental and physical practice. Reading about self-defense techniques can be meaningless if these skills are not practiced and learned. Only through practice and application can you realize that self-defense skills are not only attainable, but that they can work realistically in an attack situation. With confidence in your ability to protect yourself, you will be well on your way to avoid becoming another statistic in our violent society. Do not be vulnerable; do not become a victim of crime.

Adequate self-defense for women is more than an exercise in wishful thinking. It should be the obligation of every women—young and old alike!

About the Author

Susan L. Peterson is a free-lance writer who resides in the San Francisco Bay Area. As the first woman instructor in the history of the United States Military Academy, West Point, New York, she has appeared several times on national television, including the Johnny Carson Tonight Show. A fitness and self-defense expert, she has written several books and has been featured in several articles in national publications, including *People* magazine. The books she has authored include: *An Improved Figure Through Exercise; Self-Defense for Women—The West Point Way; The Woman's Stretching Book; The Sexy Stomach; Sexy Legs;* and *Sexy Buttocks.*

She has worked with several major urban police departments, military martial arts experts and various women's groups across the country, and is currently a self-defense consultant with The Woman's Sports Foundation.